SPECTRUM®

Hands-On
Math

Grade 2

Spectrum®

An imprint of Carson Dellosa Education
Greensboro, North Carolina

Spectrum®
An imprint of Carson Dellosa Education
P.O. Box 35665
Greensboro, NC 27425 USA

Printed in China • All rights reserved.   ISBN 978-1-4838-5766-4

01-0262012637

Table of Contents

Table of Contents, continued

Measurement and Data

Geometry

Hands-On Manipulatives

Introduction

About *Spectrum Hands-On Math*

Hands-on learning is an important aspect of educational development. Research shows that learning by doing leads to an easier understanding and a lasting comprehension of topics.

This is why *Spectrum Hands-On Math* was created—to give children the multisensory tools needed to master math. *Spectrum Hands-On Math* allows your child to roll up their sleeves and get involved in the concepts they are learning. Presented in manageable, bite-sized pieces, *Spectrum Hands-On Math* teaches all of the major topics in the math curriculum for your child's grade level. Let *Spectrum Hands-On Math* help you help your child master math standards!

Inside this kit you will find:

- Over 300 hands-on manipulatives. Cut out these manipulatives along the dashed lines to use within the lessons.

- Dry-erase pen and panels. Find four dry-erase panels full of math aids and activities. Use the dry-erase pen to complete the **Dry-Erase** activities within the lessons.

- A storage pouch for the cut-out hands-on manipulatives.

Features of *Spectrum Hands-On Math* in Every Lesson

In each two-page lesson, find the following features:

- **Lesson Introduction:** This feature is at the start of every lesson. It walks through the skill being taught step-by-step. These worked-out problems are presented with easy-to-follow visuals. As your child moves through the lesson, they can return to this point as needed to review the steps.

Introduction, continued

- **Hands-On How To** This feature is the heart of every lesson. The hands-on activities use the cut-out manipulatives from the back of the book, along with a math mat directly on the page, to get your child having fun with active involvement in the math lesson. Each hands-on activity provides a direction for open-ended practice to ensure your child will be able to keep up the practice until they master the topic!

- **Practice Mode** This feature guides your child in practicing the skills they learned in the lesson. It provides guided questions that will help your child work from the visual and hands-on examples to the type of standard exercises they are likely to see in school.

Additional Features in *Spectrum Hands-On Math*

- **Dry-Erase** This feature offers practice activities that use the dry-erase panels and pen. These exciting activities can be done over and over again to master the strategies taught in each lesson.

- **A Closer Look** This is a feature just for you! Often, parents and caretakers struggle to help their child with math. With ever-changing teaching methods, new vocabulary and tools, and new ways of explaining familiar concepts, it can be frustrating to not know how to help your child learn. This feature is here to help. **A Closer Look** defines potentially unfamiliar terms and explains their importance, offers additional ways to teach your child, and explains what skills are needed as building blocks for future math learning.

- **Answer Key:** The **Answer Key** provides the answers to the **Practice Mode** exercises.

Spectrum Hands-On Math provides everything you need to help your child be successful in second grade math and help them enjoy math now and into the future!

Addition Practice

It is important to know the answers to addition problems without counting to find the answer. You can get faster by practicing math facts.

Hands-On How To

You will need: number cards (0–9)
Draw two number cards. Put them in the boxes. Solve. Keep practicing adding number cards.

Addition Practice

Practice Mode

Add to find the sum.

1. 15 + 3	**2.** 13 + 7	**3.** 14 + 3

4. 18   **5.** 16   **6.** 12
    + 3   + 4   + 3

7. 10   **8.** 11   **9.** 17
    + 8   + 6   + 5

A Closer Look

While it is important for children to understand how addition works, it is also important for them to learn to solve addition problems quickly and correctly in their heads. When children are able to add quickly and correctly from memory, they have developed **fluency** with this skill. You can help your child by practicing with flash cards, playing board games that involve math, or doing activities like the one in this lesson.

Subtraction Practice

It is important to know the answers to subtraction problems without counting to find the answer. You can get faster by practicing math facts.

Hands-On How To

You will need: number cards (0–9)

Draw two number cards. Put them in the boxes, placing the higher number in the higher box. Solve. Keep practicing subtracting number cards.

Subtraction Practice

 Practice Mode

Subtract to find the difference.

1.	20 $-\ 7$	**2.**	17 $-\ 3$	**3.**	14 $-\ 2$
4.	18 $-\ 6$	**5.**	20 $-\ 5$	**6.**	13 $-\ 8$
7.	15 $-\ 9$	**8.**	19 $-\ 4$	**9.**	11 $-\ 7$

A Closer Look

Help your child develop **number sense** by talking often about quantities and playing number games. Start with a group of counters and cover some with your hand. Ask your child how many you covered. Or, play a version of the card game War, subtracting the lower number from the higher one on each play.

Two-Step Word Problems

Sometimes, real-life problems require you to use two steps to find the answer. You might have to add and subtract, add and add again, or subtract and subtract again.

You go to the store with $15.00. If you buy a notebook for $3.00 and a pack of crayons for $5.00, can you also buy a glue stick for $2.00?

Add to find out how much you have spent: $3.00 + $5.00 = $8.00.

Subtract to find out how much you have left: $15.00 − $8.00 = $7.00.

$7.00 > $2.00, so you have enough to buy the glue stick.

Hands-On How To

You will need: 20 apple counters
Use the apple counters to solve the two-step problem. Then, make up your own two-step problems.

You are picking apples at the orchard. You see 13 apples you want to pick, but 5 are rotten and fall off the tree. You spot 8 more you are going to pick. How many apples will you pick in all?

Two-Step Word Problems

Dry-Erase

Use the two-step problem frame to show and solve this problem: Jade has 3 bags of pretzels and 4 granola bars. She gives 3 granola bars to Eric. How many snacks does she have now? Make up and solve your own two-step word problems.

Practice Mode

Solve these two-step real-world problems.

1. Miss Angela's class was painting pictures for the classroom. Josie painted 4 pictures, Kai painted 8 pictures, and Isaac painted 5 pictures. How many pictures did they paint all together?

_____ pictures

2. Herbert reads for 20 minutes every day. First, he reads a picture book for 5 minutes, and then he reads a comic book for 11 minutes. How much more time will he spend reading?

_____ minutes

3. Lee took 9 chocolate cupcakes and 9 vanilla cupcakes to share with her friends. She brought 3 cupcakes home. How many cupcakes did her friends eat?

_____ cupcakes

Skip Counting

Skip counting by 5s, 10s, and 100s can be used to count larger numbers faster.

Count by 5s by saying numbers that end in 5 or 0 like this:
5, 10, 15, 20, 25, 30, 35, 40

Count by 10s by saying numbers that end in 0 like this:
10, 20, 30, 40, 50, 60, 70, 80

Count by 100s by saying numbers that have two 0s at the end like this:
100, 200, 300, 400, 500, 600, 700, 800

Hands-On How To

You will need: frog hopper
Use the frog hopper to practice skip counting on the number chart by 5s and 10s. If you started skip counting by 100s after 100, what numbers would your frog hop to?

5	10	15	20	25
30	35	40	45	50
55	60	65	70	75
80	85	90	95	100

Skip Counting

Dry-Erase ▷

Use the dry-erase number line to show how you can skip count by 5s, 10s, and 100s. Write a skip-counting number for each hash mark on the number line.

Practice Mode

Fill in the blanks to show what numbers come next. Look at the numbers you wrote. What patterns do you see?

1. 15, 20, 25, _____ , _____ , _____ , _____

   skip count by _____

2. 20, 30, 40, _____ , _____ , _____ , _____

   skip count by _____

3. 50, 55, 60, _____ , _____ , _____ , _____

   skip count by _____

4. 300, 400, 500, _____ , _____ , _____ , _____

   skip count by _____

Odd or Even?

Even numbers can be paired equally. Odd numbers have one left over when they are paired.

11 is an odd number.
There are 11 rabbits. 11 rabbits split into 5 pairs. 1 rabbit is left over.

| 1 | 2 | 3 | 4 | 5 |

Hands-On How To

You will need: 30 frog cut-outs
Decide if each number is odd or even by counting out the same number of frogs and putting two frogs on each lily pad. If there's a lonely frog, the number is odd. Keep showing numbers of frogs and deciding if the numbers are odd or even.

16   25   12

Odd or Even?

Dry-Erase

Use the dry-erase pad to draw objects like stars, flowers, bugs, or anything you choose to show these numbers: 12, 29, 18. Circle pairs to find if numbers are odd or even. Keep testing more numbers to see if they are odd or even.

Practice Mode

Circle pairs of shapes. Write *odd* or *even* for each number.

1. 15 _____

2. 10 _____

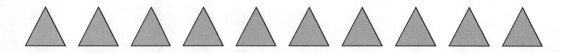

3. 22 _____

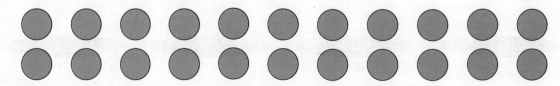

4. 17 _____

Odd or Even Clues

You can tell if a number is odd or even by thinking about counting by 2s to 10.

If a number ends in 2, 4, 6, 8, or 0, it is an even number. If the number ends in 1, 3, 5, 7, or 9, it is an odd number.

47 is an odd number because it ends in 7. 48 is an even number because it ends in 8.

Hands-On How To

You will need: 1 apple counter, number cards (0–9)
Flip the counter onto the number chart. What number did you land on? Will the number that ends in that digit be odd or even? Use the number cards to build a number with that digit at the end.

0	1	2	3	4
5	6	7	8	9

Odd or Even Clues

Dry-Erase ✏️

Use the dry-erase T-chart to sort numbers as odd or even. Is 82 odd or even? Is 49 odd or even? Make up more numbers to sort into the T-chart.

✏️ Practice Mode

Circle odd or even for each number.

1. 78

odd or even

2. 39

odd or even

3. 75

odd or even

4. 96

odd or even

5. 21

odd or even

6. 40

odd or even

7. 82

odd or even

8. 57

odd or even

Arrays

Objects can be set up so there is the same number in each row or column. This is called an **array**. When objects are set up in an array, you can use repeated addition to find the total number.

There are 3 rows and 4 columns.

To find the total number, add:

$3 + 3 + 3 + 3 = 12$

$4 + 4 + 4 = 12$

Hands-On How To

You will need: 25 star cut-outs

Use the stars to make an array to show each problem. Keep making arrays and telling the addition problem you can use to find the total number.

$3 + 3 + 3$ $5 + 5$ $2 + 2 + 2 + 2$

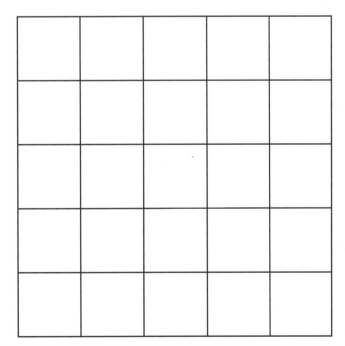

Arrays

Practice Mode

Write a repeated addition problem to show how many in each array.

1.

_____

2.

_____

3.

_____

4.

_____

5.

_____

6.

_____

A Closer Look

Rectangular arrangements of objects, called **arrays**, are one way of introducing multiplication concepts. Thinking about repeated groups of objects is a great way to get ready for multiplication problems. Use arrays to help your child explore repeated addition and then expand that understanding to multiplication facts.

Skip Counting with Arrays

When objects are set up in an array, you can skip count by the number in each column or row.

In this array, there are 2 rows and 4 columns. You can count by 4s two times to find the total number:

Hands-On How To

You will need: 25 square counters
Build arrays and skip count to find the total number. Keep making arrays and skip counting to find the total number.

4 rows of 2   3 rows of 3   4 rows of 3

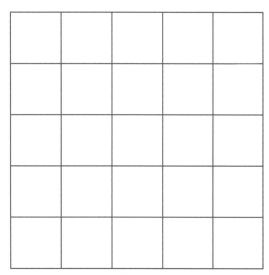

Skip Counting with Arrays

Dry-Erase

Use the dry-erase pad to draw arrays and skip count to find the total number: 5 rows of 2, 5 rows of 3.

Practice Mode

Skip count to find how many in each array.

1.    3 , 6 , _____ , _____

2.    5 , 10 , _____ , _____

3.    _____ _____ _____

4. 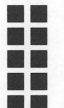   _____ _____

5. _____ _____ _____ _____

Expanded Form

Expanded form allows you to show the value of each digit in a number.

743 written in expanded form is 700 + 40 + 3.

Hands-On How To

You will need: number cards (0–9), base-ten blocks

Use the number cards to show the expanded form for each number below. Underneath, show the expanded form with base-ten blocks. Then, keep creating and expanding other numbers.

372   825   469

Hundreds		Tens		Ones
	00 +		0 +	

Expanded Form

Write each number in expanded form. Use the base-ten blocks for help.

1. 173 _____ + _____ + _____

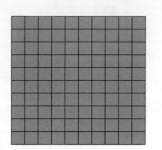 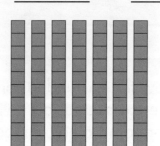

2. 298 _____ + _____ + _____

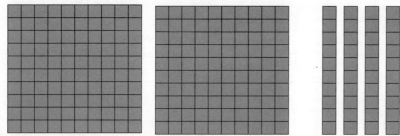 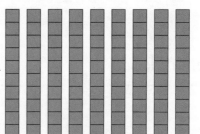 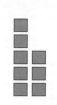

3. 327 _____ + _____ + _____

4. 726 _____ + _____ + _____

A Closer Look

When your child writes a number in **expanded form**, they are showing that they really understand place value. Many young children struggle with the concept that, in a number such as 674, the digit 6 represents 6 hundreds instead of 6 ones and the digit 7 represents 7 tens instead of 7 ones. Expanded form helps reinforce the real value of every digit in a larger number.

Number Words

Numbers can be written with numerals or number words. When you use number words, do not say *and* between the hundreds and tens places.

247 is the same as *two hundred forty-seven*.

909 is the same as *nine hundred nine*.

Hands-On How To

You will need: number cards (0–9)
Draw three number cards and place them in the spaces below. Say the number word for the number you create. Shuffle the number cards and try it again.

Hundreds	Tens	Ones

Number Words

Dry-Erase

Use the dry-erase pad with the activity on page 25. Write the number names of the numbers you create.

✎ Practice Mode

Write these numbers in word form.

1. 728 _____

2. 163 _____

Write the digits to show these numbers.

3. six hundred eighty-two

4. nine hundred thirty-seven

Addition and Subtraction with a Number Line

A number line can help you visualize addition and subtraction. You have walked 3 miles. The park is 15 miles away. How many more miles do you have left to walk?

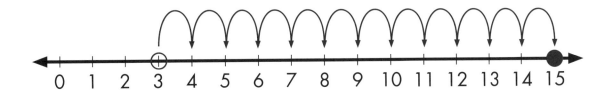

Count up from 3 to 15. How many spaces did you count? 12. You have 12 more miles to walk.

Hands-On How To

You will need: car cut-outs
Use the car cut-outs and number line to solve the problems. Then, make up your own problems to solve with the cars and number line.

A red car drives 82 miles. A blue car drives 8 miles more. How many miles does the blue car drive?

A black car drives 76 miles. A blue car drives 85 miles. How many more miles does the blue car drive?

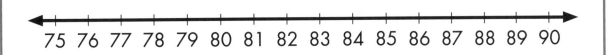

Addition and Subtraction with a Number Line

Dry-Erase

Use the dry-erase number line. Make the number line show digits 40–60.
Use the number line to solve the problems: 59 – 7, 53 – 5, 56 – 10.

Practice Mode

Use the number lines to help solve the problems.

1. Gia made $93 from the popcorn sale. Lionel made $8 less.
   How much money did Lionel make?

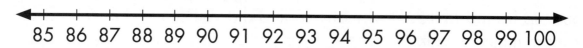

_____

2. Jay walked his dog for 75 minutes. Eleanor walked her dog for 64
   minutes. How many more minutes did Jay walk his dog than Eleanor?

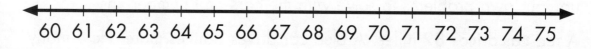

_____

3.
   Devon practiced piano for 55 minutes. Maya practiced guitar for 8
   minutes longer. How many minutes did Maya practice?

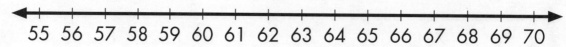

_____

Comparing Three-Digit Numbers with Base-Ten Blocks

Base-ten blocks can help you compare numbers.

327
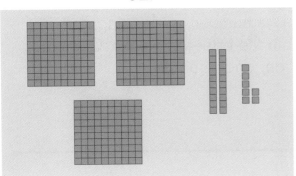

372
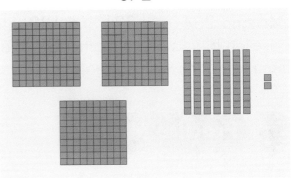

372 is greater than 327. Both numbers have an equal number of hundreds, but 372 has 7 tens and 327 only has 2 tens.

Hands-On How To

You will need: base-ten block (10 hundreds blocks, 10 tens blocks, and 10 ones blocks), equation signs (>, <, =)

Show 428 and 282 with the base-ten blocks. Compare them using the >, <, or = card. Choose more numbers to show and compare with the base-ten blocks.

Comparing Three-Digit Numbers with Base-Ten Blocks

Dry-Erase

Show these pairs of numbers in the dry-erase base-ten blocks: 138 and 173, 246 and 264, and 321 and 182. Show one number by drawing dots in the base-ten blocks and the other by coloring in the base-ten blocks. Compare them using the words *greater than*, *less than*, and *equal to*.

Practice Mode

Write the numbers shown by the base-ten blocks. Write >, <, or = to compare the numbers.

1.

_____   _____

2.

_____   _____

3.

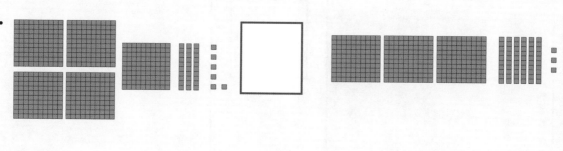

_____   _____

Comparing Three-Digit Numbers with a Place Value Chart

A place value chart can help with comparing three-digit numbers.
Compare 717 and 771.

First, compare the hundreds.
They are both 7 .

Next, compare the tens. 1 is less
than 7. You can stop here.

Hundreds	Tens	Ones
7	1	7
7	7	1

717 has fewer tens than
771, so, 717 < 771.

Hands-On How To

You will need: number cards (0–9)
Use the place value chart to build three-digit numbers and compare
them using the words *greater than, less than,* or *equal to.*

Hundreds	Tens	Ones

Comparing Three-Digit Numbers with a Place Value Chart

Dry-Erase

Use the dry-erase place value chart to compare these numbers: 371 and 284, 718 and 718. Then, build and compare your own numbers. Use the words *greater than*, *less than*, or *equal to* for comparing the numbers.

Practice Mode

Use the place value chart to compare the two numbers. Circle the words that describe the relationship.

1. 160, 601

Hundreds	Tens	Ones
1	6	0
6	0	1

greater than   less than   equal to

2. 273, 237

Hundreds	Tens	Ones
2	7	3
2	3	7

greater than   less than   equal to

3. 482, 482

Hundreds	Tens	Ones
4	8	2
4	8	2

greater than   less than   equal to

4. 402, 408

Hundreds	Tens	Ones
4	0	2
4	0	8

greater than   less than   equal to

Addition in 100

Sometimes, you need to **regroup** when you add numbers.

First, add the **ones**.   Put the **ones** in the **ones** place.   Add the **tens**.
Put the **tens** in the **tens** place.

$$\begin{array}{r} 48 \\ +\ 24 \\ \hline ? \end{array}$$
$$\begin{array}{r} 8 \\ +\ 4 \\ \hline 12 \end{array}$$
12 = 1 ten and 2 ones.

$$\begin{array}{r} 1 \\ 48 \\ +\ 24 \\ \hline 2 \end{array}$$

$$\begin{array}{r} 1 \\ 48 \\ +\ 24 \\ \hline \text{sum} = \quad 72 \end{array}$$

Hands-On How To

You will need: base-ten cookies (individual cookies, individual chocolate chips)

On each plate, use the cookies and chocolate chips to show one number in the addition problem. Count to add. Trade in 10 chocolate chips for 1 cookie with 10 chips when you need to regroup. Then, create your own addition problems.

15 + 38   49 + 28   53 + 38

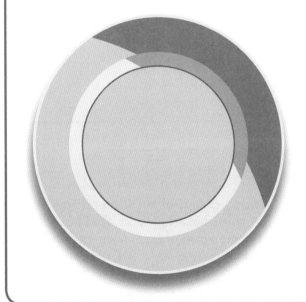

Addition in 100

Practice Mode

Color in base-ten blocks with a pencil to add with regrouping for each problem. When you have colored 10 ones, erase and fill in 1 ten.

1. 25 + 46 = _____

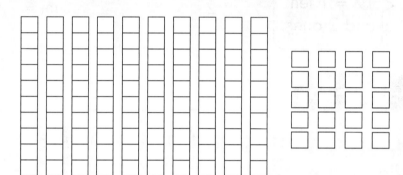

2. 36 + 35 = _____

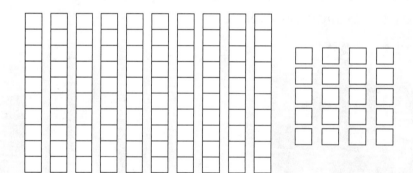

A Closer Look

Regrouping (or carrying the 1) is the math process of making groups of ten when adding. This can be a difficult concept for young children to grasp. To help, make sure your child has a firm understanding of place value first. If they don't understand the value of each numeral in a two- or three-digit number, it will be difficult for them to understand why a ten is brought over from the ones place to add to the tens digits.

Subtraction in 100

Sometimes, you need to regroup when you subtract numbers.

First, subtract the **ones**.

$$\overset{6}{\cancel{7}}2$$
$$-\,35$$

Take 1 ten from 70 to turn 2 into 12.

$$12$$
$$-\,5$$
$$\overline{7}$$

Then, subtract the **tens**.

$$6$$
$$-\,3$$
$$\overline{3}$$

Put the **ones** in the **ones** place. Put the **tens** in the **tens** place.

$$72$$
$$-\,35$$
$$\text{difference} = \overline{37}$$

Hands-On How To

You will need: base-ten blocks (10 tens and 20 ones)

Use the base-ten blocks to solve the subtraction problems. Show the bigger number with the base-ten blocks. Then, take away the smaller number. Break a ten block into ones when you need to regroup to subtract. Then, make your own problems to practice subtraction with regrouping.

$$65 - 58 \qquad 42 - 17 \qquad 31 - 27$$

Tens	Ones

Subtraction in 100

Use the dry-erase base-ten blocks to show the larger number in each problem: 64–17, 38–19. To solve, erase the blocks for the smaller number. When you need to, regroup a ten into ones in order to subtract.

Practice Mode

Color and cross out base-ten blocks to subtract with regrouping.

1. $25 - 9 =$ _____

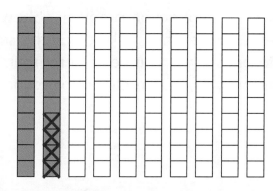

2. $36 - 18 =$ _____

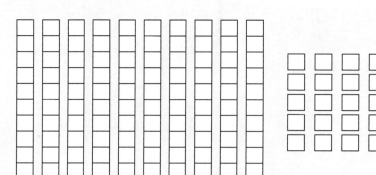

Addition and Subtraction in 100

Addition and subtraction are opposite, or **inverse**, operations. That means that one operation can be used to undo the other.

$$79 - 12 = 67 \qquad 67 + 12 = 79$$

Hands-On How To

You will need: number cards (0–9), equation signs (+, –)

Show the opposite of 36 + 28 = 64. Keep using number cards to create and show opposite equations.

Addition and Subtraction in 100

 Practice Mode

Fill in the blanks to show how addition and subtraction are opposites.

1. $44 + \underline{\hspace{2cm}} = 96$

    $96 - 44 = \underline{\hspace{2cm}}$

2. $38 + 36 = \underline{\hspace{2cm}}$

    $74 - 36 = \underline{\hspace{2cm}}$

3. $\underline{\hspace{2cm}} + 37 = 85$

    $85 - \underline{\hspace{2cm}} = 48$

4. $38 + \underline{\hspace{2cm}} = 87$

    $\underline{\hspace{2cm}} - 38 = 49$

5. $51 + \underline{\hspace{2cm}} = 72$

    $72 - \underline{\hspace{2cm}} = 21$

6. $\underline{\hspace{2cm}} + 63 = 81$

    $81 - 18 = \underline{\hspace{2cm}}$

A Closer Look

Understanding that addition and subtraction are **inverse** operations is an essential early math skill. An inverse equation is an opposite equation, or an equation that undoes the other. This understanding allows for critical thinking when solving real-world math equations. It is also an essential part of understanding multiplication and division, two more inverse operations that your child will become familiar with next year.

Word Problems

When solving word problems, it is important to decide if you need to add or subtract.

Your friend gives you **21** coins. Now, you have **39** coins. How many coins did you have to **start**?

> You are missing the **starting** number.

?	**21**	**39**
Start	**Change**	**Result**

39 – 21 = 18
You started with 18 coins.

> Remember: Subtraction undoes addition. Subtract the **change** from the **result** to find the start.

Hands-On How To

You will need: money cut-outs (pennies, dimes, nickels, quarters)

Act out the word problem by moving coins from one wallet panel to the next. Then, make up your own coin word problems to solve.

You have 10 coins after lunch. Your lunch cost 9 coins. How many coins did you have before lunch?

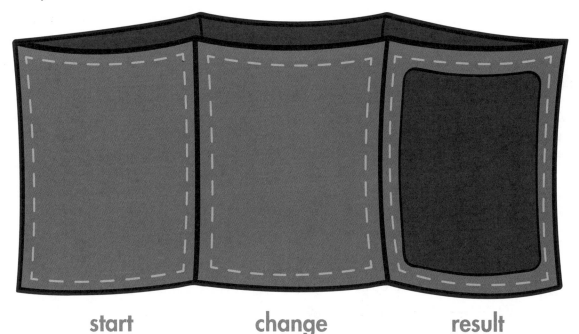

start   change   result

Word Problems

 Practice Mode

Solve each real-world word problem.

1. A school has two second grade classes. One class has 27 students. The other class has 31 students. How many second graders are there in all?

    _____ students

2. There are 63 people at the park. If 25 people are at the playground, how many people are hiking on the trails?

    _____ people

3. Aria has 12 crayons and Thomas has 15 crayons. How many crayons do they have all together?

    _____ crayons

4. There are 75 cookies on the plate. If 28 of the cookies are chocolate chip cookies, how many of the cookies are oatmeal raisin?

    _____ cookies

A Closer Look

Word problems can be difficult for children to master. They require more critical thinking than a straightforward math problem. If your child is struggling with word problems, go over these tips:

- Read the problem more than once.
- Highlight or underline any key words or numbers.
- Ignore extra information.
- Estimate what the answer might be before solving.
- Write out what the problem is asking you to find.
- Ask, does my answer make sense?

Adding More than Two Numbers

Sometimes, you will need to add more than two numbers to solve a problem. You can use the same strategy that you use with just two numbers.

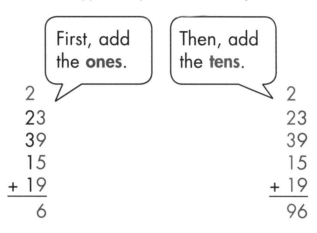

First, add the **ones**.

Then, add the **tens**.

```
   2              2
  23             23
  39             39
  15             15
+ 19           + 19
   6             96
```

Hands-On How To

You will need: number cards (0–9)
Pull 4 number cards, and set one on each side of the box. Add all the numbers you pulled together and set the answer in the middle.

Adding More than Two Numbers

Practice Mode

Solve each addition problem.

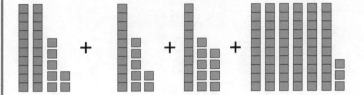

1.
$$\begin{array}{r} 27 \\ 17 \\ 19 \\ + 63 \\ \hline \end{array}$$

2.
$$\begin{array}{r} 32 \\ 27 \\ 20 \\ + 16 \\ \hline \end{array}$$

3.
$$\begin{array}{r} 53 \\ 15 \\ 29 \\ + 31 \\ \hline \end{array}$$

4.
$$\begin{array}{r} 45 \\ 28 \\ 18 \\ + 50 \\ \hline \end{array}$$

A Closer Look

A valuable skill to have when solving any kind of math problem is good math reasoning, or, in other words, the ability to look at the answer you come up with and recognize if that answer makes sense. Have your child look at the equations above. Ask them to make estimates about the problems. Will the answer be more or less than 100? Do any of the digits make tens? If the numbers were shown with coins, how many dimes and quarters would there be? By asking these questions, your child will learn to double check their answers if they don't match their initial reasoning.

Addition in 1,000

A place value chart can help you add larger numbers. Find 294 + 381.

Hundreds	Tens	Ones
1		
2	9	4
3	8	1
6	**7**	**5**

Last, add the **hundreds**.
1 + 2 + 3 = 6

First, add the **ones**.
4 + 1 = 5

Then, add the **tens**. 9 + 8 = 17
Carry the 1 to the **hundreds** column.

Hands-On How To

You will need: base-ten blocks
Use the base-ten blocks to build three-digit addition problems and solve them.

Hundreds	Tens	Ones

Addition in 1,000

Use the dry-erase place value chart to create and solve three-digit addition problems.

Practice Mode

Use the place value charts to help you add and solve these problems.

1. 372 + 284 = _____

Hundreds	Tens	Ones
3	7	2
2	8	4

2. 836 + 147 = _____

Hundreds	Tens	Ones

3. 484 + 371 = _____

Hundreds	Tens	Ones

4. 183 + 740 = _____

Hundreds	Tens	Ones

Subtraction in 1,000

A place value chart can help you subtract larger numbers. Find 846 – 281.

Hundreds	Tens	Ones
7 8̸ 2	1 4 8	6 1
5	6	5

Last, subtract the hundreds. 7 – 2 = 5

First, subtract the ones. 6 – 1 = 5

Then, subtract the tens. 4 – 8 = ? You can't subtract from a smaller number. Take 1 hundred (or 10 tens) from the hundreds column. Now, subtract 8 from 14.

Hands-On How To

You will need: base-ten blocks
Use the numbers to build three-digit subtraction problems and solve them.

Hundreds	Tens	Ones

Subtraction in 1,000

 Dry-Erase

Use the dry-erase place value chart to create and solve three-digit subtraction problems.

Practice Mode

Use the place value charts to help you subtract and solve these problems.

1. 836 – 371 = _____

Hundreds	Tens	Ones
8	3	6
3	7	1

2. 371 – 167 = _____

Hundreds	Tens	Ones

3. 937 – 226 = _____

Hundreds	Tens	Ones

4. 841 – 173 = _____

Hundreds	Tens	Ones

Multistep Word Problems

Sometimes, real-world math problems need more than one step to solve the problem.

A gumball machine has **739** pieces of **blue**, **purple**, and **red** gum. If there are **273** pieces of **blue** gum and **209** pieces of **purple** gum, how many pieces of **red** gum are in the machine?

What are you being asked to find? The amount of **red** gum.
We know that **blue** + **purple** + **red** = **739**.

First, add **blue** + **purple**.

$$\begin{array}{r} 273 \\ +\ 209 \\ \hline 482 \end{array}$$

Then, subtract **blue** and **purple** from the total.

$$\begin{array}{r} 739 \\ -\ 482 \\ \hline 257 \end{array} = \text{pieces of } \textbf{red} \text{ gum}$$

Hands-On How To

You will need: base-ten cookies (individual chocolate chips, individual cookies, and cookie trays), equation signs (+, −)

Decide what steps you need to take to solve the problem and act it out. Then, come up with your own two-step word problems about the bakery.

The bakery needs 724 cookies. They baked 264 cookies in one batch and 183 in another. How many cookies do they have left to bake?

Multistep Word Problems

 Practice Mode

Decide when to add and subtract to solve these real-life problems.

1. There are 284 students at the elementary school who play sports. There are 491 students who are in a school club. The remaining students play an instrument. If there are 906 students at the school, how many students play an instrument?

_____

2. The gym at the school can hold 500 students at one time. If there are 138 kindergartners in the gym along with 208 first graders, how many second graders can come into the gym?

_____

3. There are 187 boys and 154 girls in second grade. There are 126 second grade students in one hallway. How many second grade students are in the other hallway?

_____

4. The elementary school has 840 desks. 283 of those desks are broken, so the school buys 372 new desks. How many desks does the school have now?

_____

A Closer Look

Make sure to talk positively about math with your child. Be careful to avoid saying, "Some people just aren't good at math," or "Math is hard." Instead, encourage your child to have fun with math and reward effort. Let your child know that practice and hard work build understanding and growth. You may want to share a picture book that celebrates math, such as *On Beyond a Million: An Amazing Math Journey* by David M. Schwartz.

Measuring in Inches

Standard units of measurement allow everyone to measure an object with a ruler and get the same length. One standard unit for measuring length is the inch.

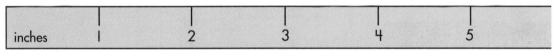

This pen is 5 inches long.

Hands-On How To

You will need: ruler cut-out
Use the ruler to find out how long each object is in inches. Then, find other objects you can measure.

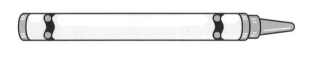

Measuring in Inches

Dry-Erase

Draw these objects beside the dry-erase ruler: a 2-inch caterpillar, a 7-inch snake.

Practice Mode

Write the length of each item.

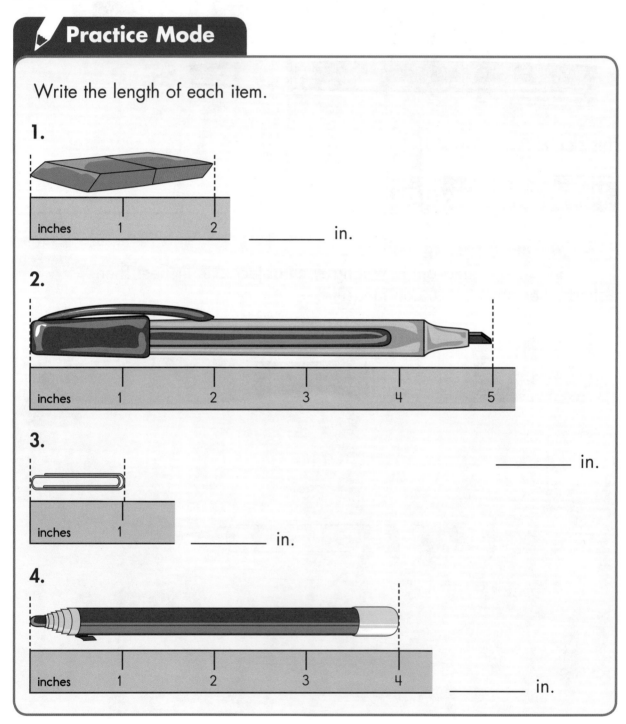

1.

inches　1　2 _____ in.

2.

inches　1　2　3　4　5

3. _____ in.

inches　1 _____ in.

4.

inches　1　2　3　4 _____ in.

Measuring in Centimeters

Another standard unit for measuring length is the centimeter.

This toothbrush is 12 centimeters long.

Hands-On How To

You will need: ruler cut-out
Use the ruler to find out how long each object is in centimeters. Then, find other objects you can measure.

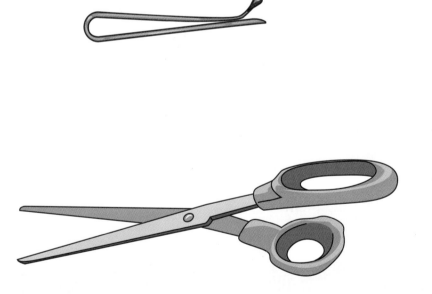

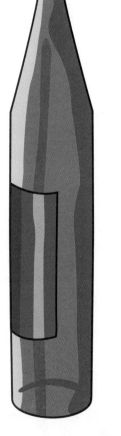

Measuring in Centimeters

Dry-Erase ✏

Draw these objects beside the dry-erase ruler: a 7-centimeter bug,
a 3-centimeter fish.

✏ Practice Mode

Write the length of each item.

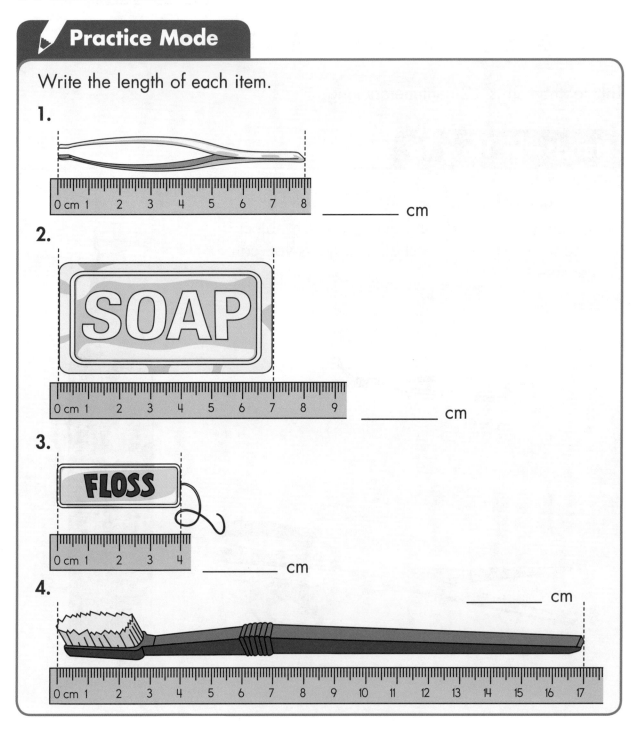

1.

_____ cm

2.

_____ cm

3.

_____ cm

4.

_____ cm

Comparing Units of Measurement

The length of an object can be measured using inches and centimeters.

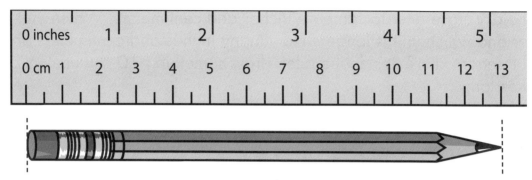

This pencil is 13 centimeters, or about 5 inches, long.

Hands-On How To

You will need: ruler cut-out

Use the ruler to find out how long each object is in both centimeters and inches. Tell if centimeters or inches give you a more accurate measurement. Then, find more objects to measure in centimeters and inches.

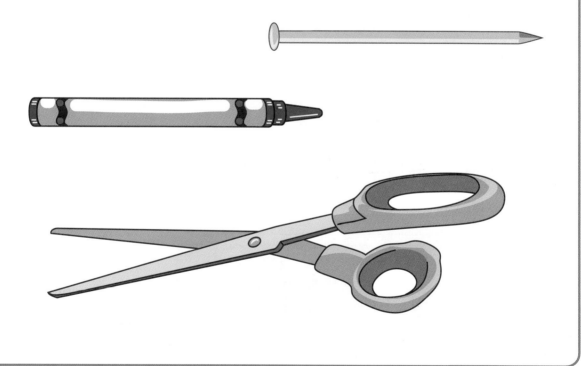

Comparing Units of Measurement

Dry-Erase

Use the dry-erase ruler to compare inches and centimeters. Which unit is shorter and which unit is longer? How many inches and centimeters are equal to each other? Beside the ruler, draw something 10 centimeters or 4 inches long.

Practice Mode

Tell the length of each item to the closest centimeter and inch.

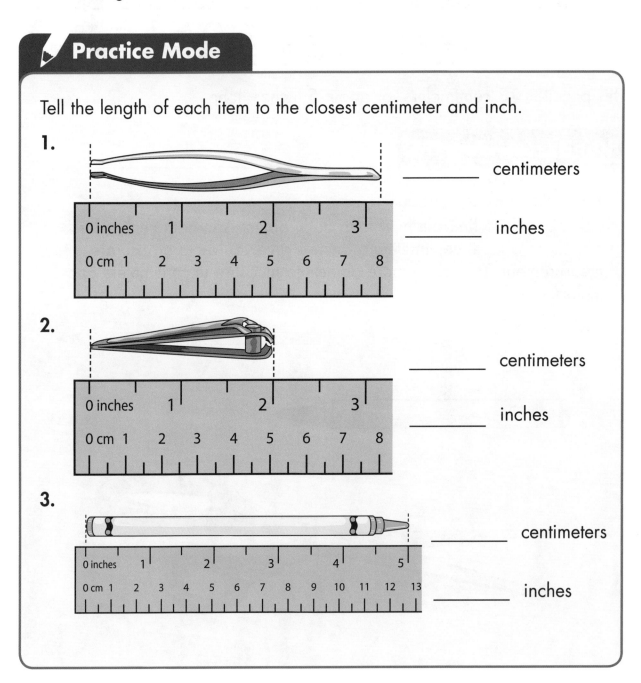

1. _____ centimeters

_____ inches

2. _____ centimeters

_____ inches

3. _____ centimeters

_____ inches

Estimate Length

Sometimes, a ruler isn't available when something needs to be measured. You can use your eyes and your knowledge of measurement to **estimate** how long something is.

This paper clip is about 2 inches long.

Hands-On How To

You will need: ruler cut-out

Estimate the length of each object in inches. Then, check to see how close you were. Find other objects and estimate their length. Check their actual length with the ruler.

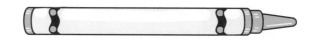

Estimate Length

Practice Mode

Estimate the length of each object in inches.

1.

about _____ inches

2.

about _____ inches

3.

about _____ inches

4.

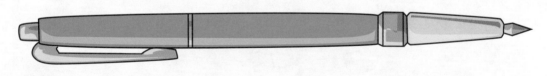

about _____ inches

A Closer Look

Making and checking **estimates** is a good way to help your child develop math reasoning skills. Challenge your child to build on what they know to solve new problems. For example, ask, "You know that a piece of paper is about 11 inches tall. Is the windowsill longer than a piece of paper? About how long is the windowsill?"

Comparing Length with Inches

You can compare the length of two objects by finding the difference between their measurements.

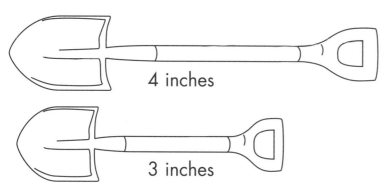

4 inches

3 inches

4 inches – 3 inches = 1 inch
The first shovel is 1 inch longer than the second shovel.

Hands-On How To

You will need: object cut-outs (toothbrush, soap, tweezers, nail clippers)

Measure the length of each object in inches. Subtract to find the difference between them. Find more objects to measure and compare.

| inches | 1 | 2 | 3 | 4 | 5 | 6 |

Comparing Length with Inches

Dry-Erase

Use the dry-erase ruler. Beside it, draw a line that is 4 inches long. Draw another line that is 2 inches longer. Draw a line that is 3 inches. Draw another line that is 3 inches longer.

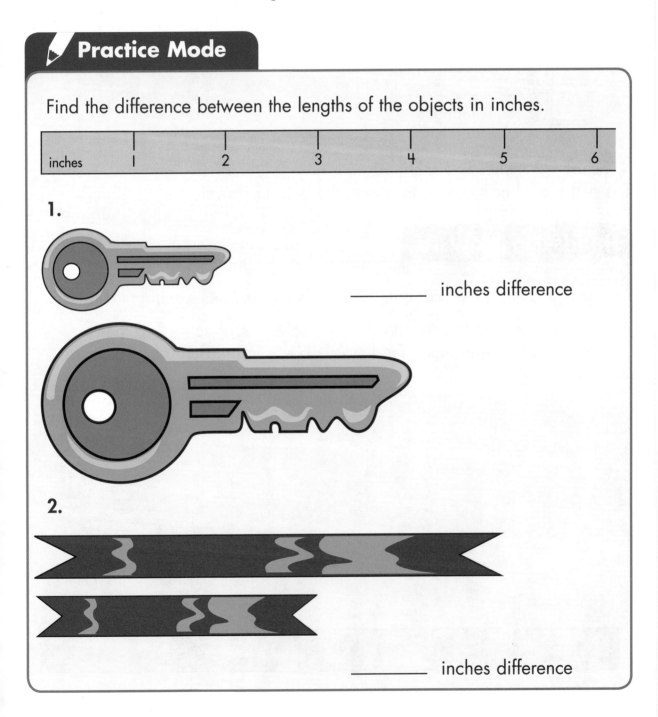

Practice Mode

Find the difference between the lengths of the objects in inches.

inches	1	2	3	4	5	6

1.

_____ inches difference

2.

_____ inches difference

Comparing Length with Centimeters

You can compare the length of two objects by finding the difference between their measurements.

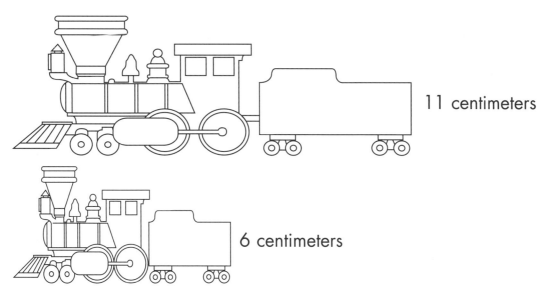

11 centimeters

6 centimeters

11 centimeters − 6 centimeters = 5 centimeters

Hands-On How To

You will need: object cut-outs (toothbrush, soap, tweezers, nail clippers) Measure the length of each object in centimeters. Subtract to find the difference between them. Find more objects to measure and compare.

Comparing Length with Centimeters

Dry-Erase

Use the dry-erase ruler. Beside it, draw a line that is 8 centimeters long. Draw another line that is 3 centimeters shorter. Draw a line that is 13 centimeters long. Draw another line that is 4 centimeters longer.

Practice Mode

Tell the difference between the lengths of the objects.

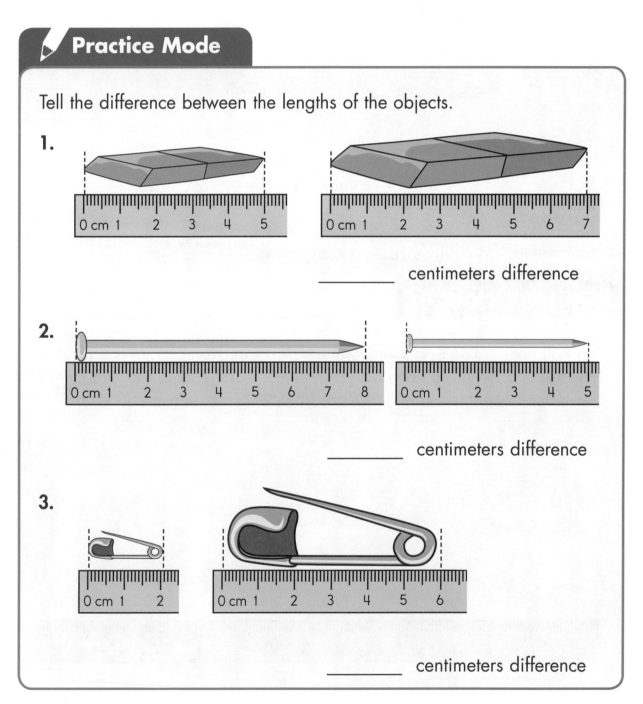

1.

_____ centimeters difference

2.

_____ centimeters difference

3.

_____ centimeters difference

Real-World Length Problems

Length is an example of how numbers are used in the real world. Sometimes, real-world problems will include adding or subtracting different lengths.

Tia's bike is 5 feet long. Mike's bike is 4 feet long. They need to store the bikes in an alley that is 11 feet long. Will both bikes fit?

First, add the length of the two bikes: 5 + 4 = 9.
Then, compare 11 and 9. 11 is greater than 9. Both bikes will fit.

Hands-On How To

You will need: car cut-outs
Solve the problem using the car cut-outs. Then, make up other real-world problems with cars and parking lanes.

A parking lane is 25 feet long. If a car is 5 feet long, how many cars can fit in the parking lane?

Real-World Length Problems

Dry-Erase 🖊

Use the two-step equation frame to show how to solve this problem: A bookshelf is 48 inches wide. If a tray that is 20 inches wide is already on the shelf, how much space is left for books?

✏ Practice Mode

Solve each real-world length problem. Explain the math when needed.

1. Mike and Jen were throwing baseballs at recess. They decided to see who could throw farther. Mike threw the ball 36 inches and Jen threw the ball 42 inches. How much farther did Jen throw the ball?

   _____ inches

2. A puzzle is supposed to be 75 centimeters wide after it is put together. So far, it is 12 centimeters wide. How much more is left to be put together?

   _____ centimeters

3. Pablo has a pool that is 25 feet long. He has 3 floats that are 6 feet long each. Will they all fit end-to-end in his pool?

   _____

4. Josephine is 100 centimeters tall. How many 30-centimeter steps will she need to stand on to reach a shelf that is 200 centimeters tall?

   _____ steps

Using a Line Plot

A line plot is used for recording data.

This line plot shows 8 data points for the height, in inches, of 8 second graders. Each dot represents one second grader.

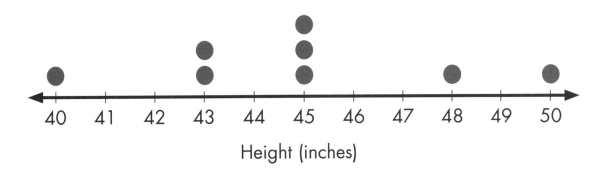

Height (inches)

Hands-On How To

You will need: ruler, cut-outs, 6 square counters, object cut-outs (paintbrush, toothbrush, soap, tweezers, nail clippers), car cut-out

Measure each object in inches. Use a counter to mark the line plot. Then, measure other things you see and make another line plot.

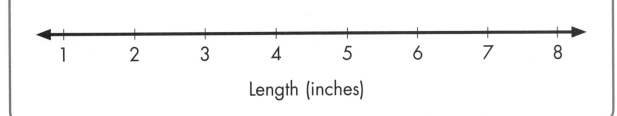

Length (inches)

Using a Line Plot

Dry-Erase

Measure the length of things you find around the room to the nearest inch. Create a line plot by marking a data point for each object above the dry-erase number line.

Practice Mode

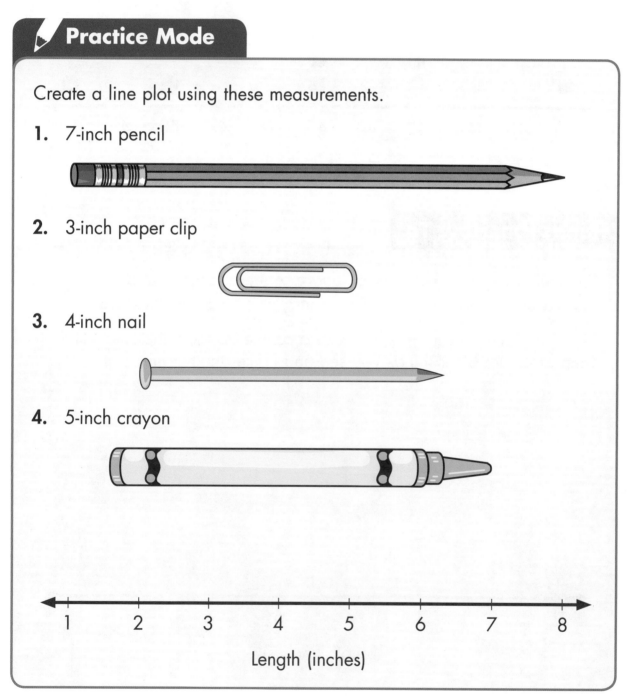

Create a line plot using these measurements.

1. 7-inch pencil

2. 3-inch paper clip

3. 4-inch nail

4. 5-inch crayon

1   2   3   4   5   6   7   8

Length (inches)

Using a Pictograph

A pictograph uses simple pictures to show data. This graph shows that Sarah saw 3 frogs, 5 ducks, 2 birds, and 6 fish when she went to the pond.

Animals at the Pond

frogs	🐸	🐸	🐸			
ducks	🦆	🦆	🦆	🦆	🦆	
birds	🐦	🐦				
fish	🐟	🐟	🐟	🐟	🐟	🐟

Hands-On How To

You will need: object cut-outs (baseballs, books, plants, paintbrushes)
Use the cut-outs to create a pictograph. Ask family and friends if they like sports, reading, art, or gardening best. Record your data with the object cut-outs.

Favorite Activities

sports					
reading					
art					
gardening					

Using a Pictograph

Dry-Erase

Collect some data and use the blank dry-erase graph to make your own pictograph. Some examples: types of pets, favorite foods, favorite movies.

Practice Mode

Complete the pictograph below. Draw simple pictures that show the kind of weather for each day: 6 rainy days, 10 sunny days, 4 snowy days, 6 cloudy days.

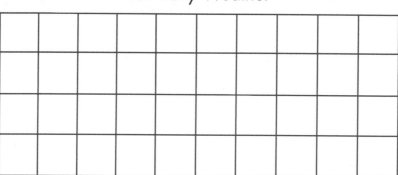

February Weather

rainy days

sunny days

snowy days

cloudy days

1. How many days was the weather recorded? _____

2. How many more days were sunny than rainy? _____

3. Which kind of weather happened the least? _____

4. Which kind of weather happened the most? _____

Using a Bar Graph

Bar graphs show data using bars. This bar graph shows the number of pets from Amaya's class. 6 people have dogs, 8 people have cats, 5 people have fish, 2 people have turtles, and 4 people don't have a pet.

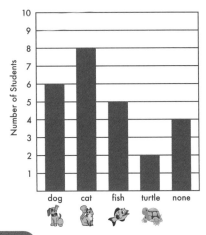

Hands-On How To

You will need: 15 square counters

Place the square counters in the bar graph to show what people had for breakfast: 7 had eggs, 3 had yogurt, 6 had cereal, and 4 had toast. Then, gather your own data by asking friends and family.

8
7
6
5
4
3
2
1
0

eggs   yogurt   cereal   toast

Using a Bar Graph

Dry-Erase

Take a look around the room. Find things that are different shapes, like circles, rectangles, triangles, and squares. Then, use the blank dry-erase graph to make a bar graph to show how many of each shape you find.

Practice Mode

Answer the questions about the bar graph.

The cafeteria at school serves different kinds of food each day. Kids buy lunch if they like what the cafeteria is serving.

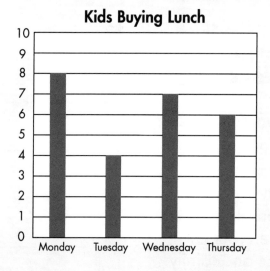

Kids Buying Lunch

1. How many kids bought lunch on Monday and Tuesday?

   _____

2. How many kids bought lunch on Wednesday and Thursday?

   _____

3. Which day had the most kids buying lunch?

   _____

4. What is the difference between the most popular lunch day and the least?

   _____

Telling Time with an Analog Clock

An analog clock is separated into 5-minute increments based on the numbers on the clock. You can find the minutes on an analog clock by counting by 5s until you get to the minute hand.

This analog clock shows 7:20.

Hands-On How To

You will need: minute hand, hour hand
Show the times on the analog clock. Then, make the clock show more times that end in 5 or 0.

2:15

7:40

9:45

Telling Time with an Analog Clock

Draw hands on the analog dry-erase clock to make these times: 3:40, 5:55, 12:25.

Practice Mode

Draw hands on the clock to show each time.

1. 10:15

2. 7:05

3. 2:50

4. 1:55

Telling Time with a Digital Clock

A digital clock tells time with digits.

This digital clock shows 7:20.

Hands-On How To

You will need: number cards (0–9)
Show the times from the analog clocks on the digital clock.
Then, make the clock show more times that end in 5 or 0.

Telling Time with a Digital Clock

Show the times on the digital dry-erase clock: 8:20, 2:30, 7:45.

Practice Mode

Show the time from the analog clock on the digital clock.

1.

2.

3.

4.

Adding and Subtracting with Dollars and Coins

When working with money, you need to know the value of each coin and bill.

A penny is worth 1¢.   A nickel is worth 5¢.

A dime is worth 10¢.   A quarter is worth 25¢.

A dollar  is worth $1.00.

Hands-On How To

You will need: money cut-outs (pennies, nickels, dimes, quarters, dollars), equation signs (+, −, =)

Add or subtract to find out how much money in dollars and cents. Place the correct equation signs in the boxes. Keep putting together and taking apart groups of money to see how much you have.

3 quarters + 2 dimes   1 dime − 2 nickels   1 dollar + 1 penny

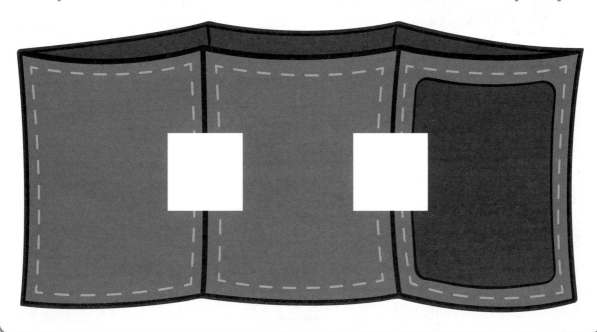

Adding and Subtracting with Dollars and Coins

Dry-Erase ✏

Solve the problem on the dry-erase pad. Draw the money you have left.
You have $1.00 to spend at the store. You spend 25¢ on a piece of gum
and 50¢ on a pack of crackers. How much money do you have left?

Practice Mode

Add or subtract to find how many dollars and cents you have.

1. 25¢ 10¢ 10¢ 10¢ 5¢ 5¢

   1 quarter   + 3 dimes   + 2 nickles   _____

2. $1   25¢   25¢   25¢

   1 dollar   + 3 quarters   _____

3. 3 dimes + 6 quarters _____

4. 2 dollars – 2 quarters – 5 dimes _____

5. 1 dollar + 6 nickels – 1 quarter _____

6. 10 dimes + 4 quarters _____

Money Word Problems

Solving real-world math problems about money is an important life skill.

Marta has $1.35. If she buys a milk that costs 75¢, how much money will she have left?

$$\begin{aligned} \$1.35 \\ -\ \underline{\$0.75} \\ \$0.60 \end{aligned}$$

Hands-On How To

You will need: money cut-outs (dollars, quarters, dimes, nickels, pennies)
You have $5.00. You want to buy a teddy bear and a baseball card. Do you have enough money? What other combinations can you buy with $5.00?

Money Word Problems

Practice Mode

Add and subtract to find the answers to the word problems.

$1	25¢	10¢	5¢	1¢

1. Jada has 3 dollars, 4 quarters, 6 dimes, and 7 pennies. If she buys a bag of chips for $1.45, how much money will she have left?

   _____

2. Malik goes to the store with $7.82. He buys candy for $2.15 and juice for $1.59. How much money will Malik have left?

   _____

3. Tiana has $4.00. She wants to buy a book that costs $3.50 and a toy that costs $2.75. How much more money will Tiana need to buy the book and the toy?

   _____

A Closer Look

If you often use a debit or credit card to make purchases, your child may be unfamiliar with using cash. Foster math skills by allowing your child to buy things at the store using bills and coins. Encourage your child to verify that the right amount of change was given. You may wish to provide a small cash allowance for your child that encourages thinking about spending and saving.

Quadrilaterals

A quadrilateral is a closed shape with four sides. These shapes are all quadrilaterals.

  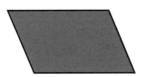 

Hands-On How To

You will need: shape cut-outs (rectangle, square, rhombus, parallelogram, trapezoid)

Match the quadrilaterals to their correct shapes below. Name them. Explain what makes each shape a quadrilateral. Then, practice matching the shapes to things you see around you.

Quadrilaterals

Use the dry-erase dot grid to draw quadrilaterals.

Practice Mode

Color the quadrilaterals.

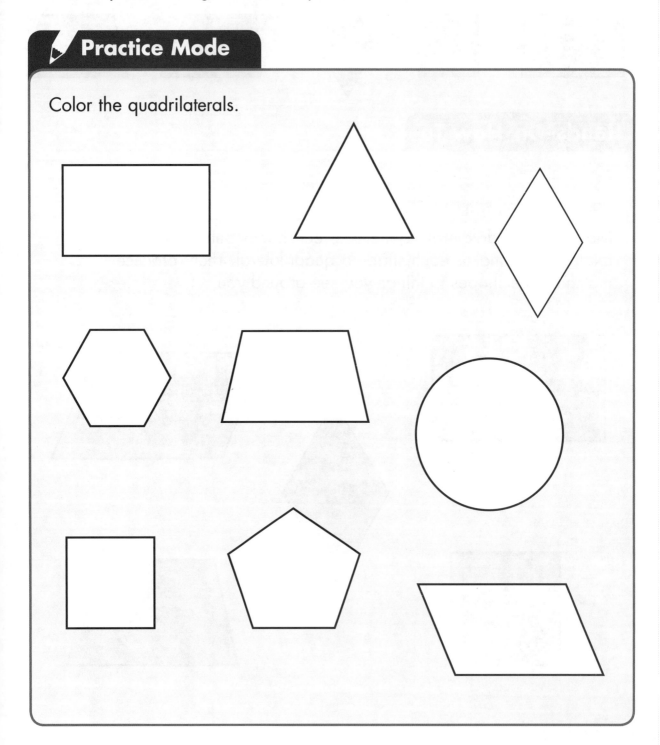

Other Shapes

A triangle has 3 sides and 3 angles. A pentagon has 5 sides and 5 angles. A hexagon has 6 sides and 6 angles. A cube has 6 square faces.

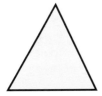  

Hands-On How To

You will need: shape cut-outs (triangles, pentagons, hexagons), cube net

Assemble the cube. Stack the shapes in all the bubbles they belong to.

3 sides   **5 sides**   **6 sides**

2-D shapes   **3-D shapes**   **closed shapes**

Other Shapes

Use the dry-erase dot grid to draw one of each: triangle, pentagon, hexagon, cube.

Practice Mode

Fill in the missing information for each shape.

1. triangle: 3 _____, 3 angles

2. cube: 3-D shape, 6 _____ faces

3. _____ : 5 sides, 5 angles

4. hexagon: 6 _____, 6 _____

Draw the shapes.

5. hexagon

6. triangle

Label the shapes.

7.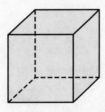

    _____

8.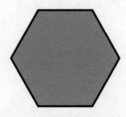

    _____

Area Concepts

Rectangles can be divided into equal-size squares. You can describe the size of a rectangle by telling how many squares are in each row and column.

This rectangle is 3 rows of squares high and 5 columns of squares long. It has 15 total squares.

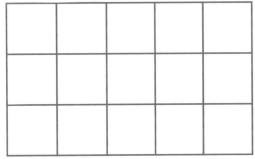

Hands-On How To

You will need: 3 rectangle cut-outs

Place the rectangle cut-outs on the graph paper. Trace each rectangle. Tell how many rows and columns of squares fit inside each rectangle.

Area Concepts

Dry-Erase

Use the dry-erase dot grid to draw rectangles of different sizes. Then, use the dots to draw equal size squares inside each rectangle and tell how many squares fit.

Practice Mode

Solve the multiplication problems. Count the total number of squares for help. The first one has been done for you.

1.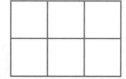

2 x 3 = 6

2.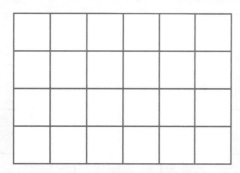

6 x 4 = _____

3.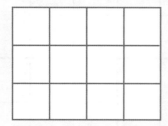

_____ x _____ = 12

4.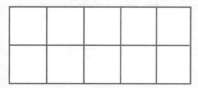

_____ x _____ = _____

Fractions with Circles

Circles can be divided into equal parts, or fractions.

 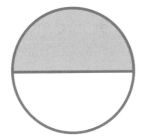 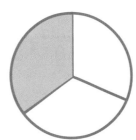 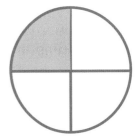

This is a whole. This is $\frac{1}{2}$. This is $\frac{1}{3}$. This is $\frac{1}{4}$.

Hands-On How To

You will need: circle fraction cut-outs (halves, thirds, fourths)

Use the circle cut-outs. Show these fractions: $\frac{1}{4}$, $\frac{2}{4}$, $\frac{3}{4}$, $\frac{4}{4}$.

Keep showing circle fractions using the cut-outs and describing those fractions by their names.

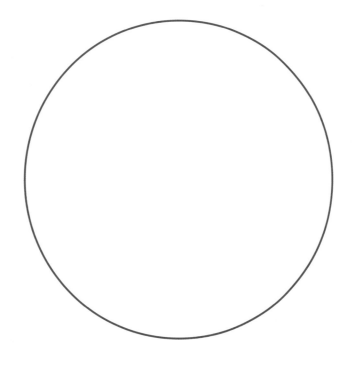

Fractions with Circles

Dry-Erase ✏

Draw a circle on the dry-erase pad. Draw lines through the circle to make fractions. Name the fractions.

✏ Practice Mode

Shade each circle as described.

1. Show $\frac{3}{4}$.

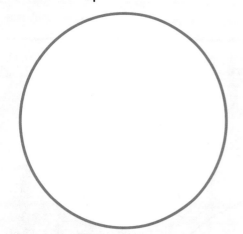

2. Show $\frac{1}{2}$.

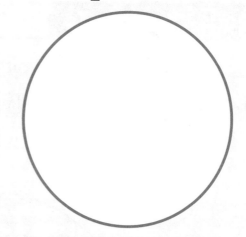

3. Show $\frac{1}{3}$.

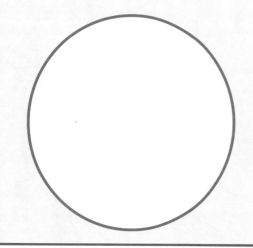

4. Show $\frac{3}{3}$.

Fractions with Rectangles

Rectangles can be divided into equal parts, or fractions.

This is $\frac{1}{2}$.　　　　This is $\frac{1}{3}$.　　　　This is $\frac{1}{4}$.

Hands-On How To

You will need: rectangle fraction cut-outs (halves, thirds, fourths)

Use the rectangle cut-outs. Show $\frac{1}{3}$, $\frac{2}{3}$, and $\frac{3}{3}$.

Keep showing rectangle fractions using the cut-outs and describing those fractions by their names.

Fractions with Rectangles

Dry-Erase

Draw a rectangle on the dry-erase pad. Draw lines through the rectangle to divide it equally into fractions. Name the fractions.

Practice Mode

Shade each rectangle as described.

1. Show $\frac{1}{3}$.

2. Show $\frac{3}{4}$.

3. Show $\frac{2}{4}$.

4. Show $\frac{2}{2}$.

Write the fraction each rectangle is showing.

5.

_____

6.

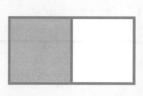

_____

Addition Practice

Practice Mode

Add to find the sum.

1.   15
  + 3
18
	2. 13
	  + 7
	20
		3. 14
		  + 3
		17

4.   18
  + 3
21
	5. 16
	  + 4
	20
		6. 12
		  + 3
		15

7.   10
  + 8
18
	8. 11
	  + 6
	17
		9. 17
		  + 5
		22

A Closer Look

While it is important for children to understand how addition works, it is also important for them to learn to solve addition problems quickly and correctly in their heads. When children are able to add quickly and correctly from memory, they have developed **fluency** with this skill. You can help your child by practicing with flash cards, playing board games that involve math, or doing activities like the one in this lesson.

Subtraction Practice

Practice Mode

Subtract to find the difference.

1.   20
  − 7
13
	2. 17
	  − 3
	14
		3. 14
		  − 2
		12

4.   18
  − 6
12
	5. 20
	  − 5
	15
		6. 13
		  − 8
		5

7.   15
  − 9
6
	8. 19
	  − 4
	15
		9. 11
		  − 7
		4

A Closer Look

Help your child develop **number sense** by talking often about quantities and playing number games. Start with a group of counters and cover some with your hand. Ask your child how many you covered. Or, play a version of the card game War, subtracting the lower number from the higher one on each play.

Two-Step Word Problems

Dry-Erase

Use the two-step problem frame to show and solve this problem: Jade has 3 bags of pretzels and 4 granola bars. She gives 3 granola bars to Eric. How many snacks does she have now? Make up and solve your own two-step word problems.

Practice Mode

Solve these two-step real-world problems.

1. Miss Angela's class was painting pictures for the classroom. Josie painted 4 pictures, Kai painted 8 pictures, and Isaac painted 5 pictures. How many pictures did they paint all together?

    17 pictures

2. Herbert reads for 20 minutes every day. First, he reads a picture book for 5 minutes, and then he reads a comic book for 11 minutes. How much more time will he spend reading?

    4 minutes

3. Lee took 9 chocolate cupcakes and 9 vanilla cupcakes to share with her friends. She brought 3 cupcakes home. How many cupcakes did her friends eat?

    15 cupcakes

Skip Counting

Dry-Erase

Use the dry-erase number line to show how you can skip count by 5s, 10s, and 100s. Write a skip-counting number for each hash mark on the number line.

Practice Mode

Fill in the blanks to show what numbers come next. Look at the numbers you wrote. What patterns do you see?

1. 15, 20, 25, **30**, **35**, **40**, **45**

    skip count by **5**

2. 20, 30, 40, **50**, **60**, **70**, **80**

    skip count by **10**

3. 50, 55, 60, **65**, **70**, **75**, **80**

    skip count by **5**

4. 300, 400, 500, **600**, **700**, **800**, **900**

    skip count by **100**

Odd or Even?

Dry-Erase

Use the dry-erase pad to draw objects like stars, flowers, bugs, or anything you choose to show these numbers: 12, 29, 18. Circle pairs to find if numbers are odd or even. Keep testing more numbers to see if they are odd or even.

Practice Mode

Circle pairs of shapes. Write *odd* or *even* for each number.

1. 15 __odd__

2. 10 __even__

3. 22 __even__

4. 17 __odd__

Odd or Even Clues

Dry-Erase

Use the dry-erase T-chart to sort numbers as odd or even. Is 82 odd or even? Is 49 odd or even? Make up more numbers to sort into the T-chart.

Practice Mode

Circle odd or even for each number.

1. 78   odd or (even)
2. 39   (odd) or even
3. 75   (odd) or even
4. 96   odd or (even)
5. 21   (odd) or even
6. 40   odd or (even)
7. 82   odd or (even)
8. 57   (odd) or even

Arrays

Practice Mode

Write a repeated addition problem to show how many in each array.

Answers may vary. Sample answers:

1. $5 + 5 + 5 = 15$
2. $2 + 2 + 2 + 2 = 8$
3. $5 + 5 + 5 + 5 + 5 = 25$
4. $4 + 4 + 4 + 4 + 4 = 20$
5. $6 + 6 = 12$
6. $8 + 8 + 8 = 24$

A Closer Look

Rectangular arrangements of objects, called **arrays**, are one way of introducing multiplication concepts. Thinking about repeated groups of objects is a great way to get ready for multiplication problems. Use arrays to help your child explore repeated addition and then expand that understanding to multiplication facts.

Skip Counting with Arrays

Dry-Erase

Use the dry-erase pad to draw arrays and skip count to find the total number: 5 rows of 2, 5 rows of 3.

Practice Mode

Skip count to find how many in each array.

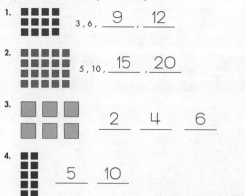

1. 3, 6, __9__, __12__
2. 5, 10, __15__, __20__
3. __2__ __4__ __6__
4. __5__ __10__
5. __2__ __4__ __6__ __8__ __10__

Expanded Form

Practice Mode

Write each number in expanded form. Use the base-ten blocks for help.

1. 173   100 + 70 + 3

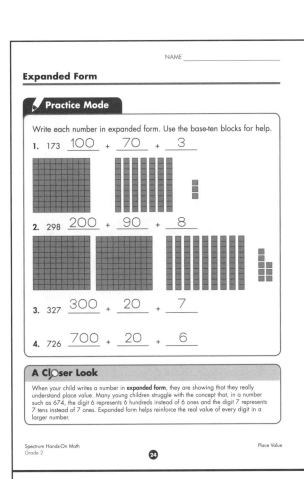

2. 298   200 + 90 + 8

3. 327   300 + 20 + 7

4. 726   700 + 20 + 6

A Closer Look

When your child writes a number in **expanded form**, they are showing that they really understand place value. Many young children struggle with the concept that, in a number such as 674, the digit 6 represents 6 hundreds instead of 6 ones and the digit 7 represents 7 tens instead of 7 ones. Expanded form helps reinforce the real value of every digit in a larger number.

Number Words

Dry-Erase

Use the dry-erase pad with the activity on page 25. Write the number names of the numbers you create.

Practice Mode

Write these numbers in word form.

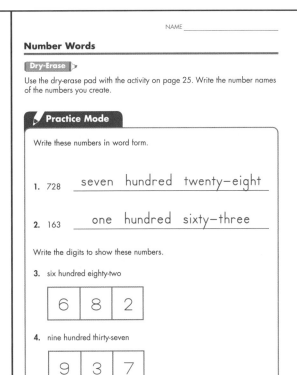

1. 728   seven hundred twenty-eight

2. 163   one hundred sixty-three

Write the digits to show these numbers.

3. six hundred eighty-two

6	8	2

4. nine hundred thirty-seven

9	3	7

Addition and Subtraction with a Number Line

Dry-Erase

Use the dry-erase number line. Make the number line show digits 40–60. Use the number line to solve the problems: 59 – 7, 53 – 5, 56 – 10.

Practice Mode

Use the number lines to help solve the problems.

1. Gia made $93 from the popcorn sale. Lionel made $8 less. How much money did Lionel make?

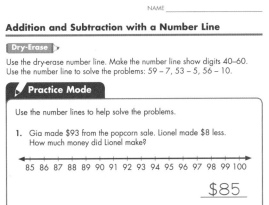

85 86 87 88 89 90 91 92 93 94 95 96 97 98 99 100

$85

2. Jay walked his dog for 75 minutes. Eleanor walked her dog for 64 minutes. How many more minutes did Jay walk his dog than Eleanor?

60 61 62 63 64 65 66 67 68 69 70 71 72 73 74 75

11

3. Devon practiced piano for 55 minutes. Maya practiced guitar for 8 minutes longer. How many minutes did Maya practice?

55 56 57 58 59 60 61 62 63 64 65 66 67 68 69 70

63

Comparing Three-Digit Numbers with Base-Ten Blocks

Dry-Erase

Show these pairs of numbers in the dry-erase base-ten blocks: 138 and 173, 246 and 264, and 321 and 182. Show one number by drawing dots in the base-ten blocks and the other by coloring in the base-ten blocks. Compare them using the words *greater than*, *less than*, and *equal to*.

Practice Mode

Write the numbers shown by the base-ten blocks. Write >, <, or = to compare the numbers.

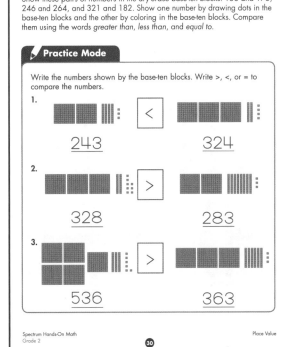

1.   243   <   324

2.   328   >   283

3.   536   >   363

NAME _____

Comparing Three-Digit Numbers with a Place Value Chart

Dry-Erase

Use the dry-erase place value chart to compare these numbers: 371 and 284, 718 and 718. Then, build and compare your own numbers. Use the words *greater than*, *less than*, or *equal to* for comparing the numbers.

Practice Mode

Use the place value chart to compare the two numbers. Circle the words that describe the relationship.

1. 160, 601

Hundreds	Tens	Ones
1	6	0
6	0	1

greater than (less than) equal to

2. 273, 237

Hundreds	Tens	Ones
2	7	3
2	3	7

(greater than) less than equal to

3. 482, 482

Hundreds	Tens	Ones
4	8	2
4	8	2

greater than less than (equal to)

4. 402, 408

Hundreds	Tens	Ones
4	0	2
4	0	8

greater than (less than) equal to

Spectrum Hands-On Math
Grade 2

32

Place Value

NAME _____

Addition in 100

Practice Mode

Color in base-ten blocks with a pencil to add with regrouping for each problem. When you have colored 10 ones, erase and fill in 1 ten.

1. 25 + 46 = __71__

2. 36 + 35 = __71__

A Closer Look

Regrouping (or carrying the 1) is the math process of making groups of ten when adding. This can be a difficult concept for young children to grasp. To help, make sure your child has a firm understanding of place value first. If they don't understand the value of each numeral in a two- or three-digit number, it will be difficult for them to understand why a ten is brought over from the ones place to add to the tens digits.

Spectrum Hands-On Math
Grade 2

34

Place Value

NAME _____

Subtraction in 100

Dry-Erase

Use the dry-erase base-ten blocks to show the larger number in each problem: 64–17, 38–19. To solve, erase the blocks for the smaller number. When you need to, regroup a ten into ones in order to subtract.

Practice Mode

Color and cross out base-ten blocks to subtract with regrouping.

1. 25 – 9 = __16__

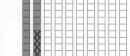

2. 36 – 18 = __18__

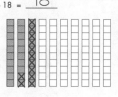

Spectrum Hands-On Math
Grade 2

36

Place Value

NAME _____

Addition and Subtraction in 100

Practice Mode

Fill in the blanks to show how addition and subtraction are opposites.

1. 44 + __52__ = 96

96 – 44 = __52__

2. 38 + 36 = __74__

74 – 36 = __38__

3. __48__ + 37 = 85

85 – __37__ = 48

4. 38 + __49__ = 87

__87__ – 38 = 49

5. 51 + __21__ = 72

72 – __51__ = 21

6. __18__ + 63 = 81

81 – 18 = __63__

A Closer Look

Understanding that addition and subtraction are **inverse** operations is an essential early math skill. An inverse equation is an opposite equation, or an equation that undoes the other. This understanding allows for critical thinking when solving real-world math equations. It is also an essential part of understanding multiplication and division, two more inverse operations that your child will become familiar with next year.

Spectrum Hands-On Math
Grade 2

38

Place Value

Spectrum Hands-On Math
Grade 2

90

Answer Key

NAME _____

Word Problems

Practice Mode

Solve each real-world word problem.

1. A school has two second grade classes. One class has 27 students. The other class has 31 students. How many second graders are there in all?
   58 students

2. There are 63 people at the park. If 25 people are at the playground, how many people are hiking on the trails?
   38 people

3. Aria has 12 crayons and Thomas has 15 crayons. How many crayons do they have all together?
   27 crayons

4. There are 75 cookies on the plate. If 28 of the cookies are chocolate chip cookies, how many of the cookies are oatmeal raisin?
   47 cookies

A Clser Look

Word problems can be difficult for children to master. They require more critical thinking than a straightforward math problem. If your child is struggling with word problems, go over these tips:

- Read the problem more than once.
- Highlight or underline any key words or numbers.
- Ignore extra information.
- Estimate what the answer might be before solving.
- Write out what the problem is asking you to find.
- Ask, does my answer make sense?

NAME _____

Adding More than Two Numbers

Practice Mode

Solve each addition problem.

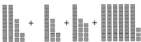

1.   27
      17
      19
    + 63
    126

2.   32
      27
      20
    + 16
    95

3.   53
      15
      29
    + 31
    128

4.   45
      28
      18
    + 50
    141

A Clser Look

A valuable skill to have when solving any kind of math problem is good math reasoning, or, in other words, the ability to look at the answer you come up with and recognize if that answer makes sense. Have your child look at the equations above. Ask them to make estimates about the problems. Will the answer be more or less than 100? Do any of the digits make tens? If the numbers were shown with coins, how many dimes and quarters would there be? By asking these questions, your child will learn to double check their answers if they don't match their initial reasoning.

NAME _____

Addition in 1,000

Dry-Erase

Use the dry-erase place value chart to create and solve three-digit addition problems.

Practice Mode

Use the place value charts to help you add and solve these problems.

1. 372 + 284 = **656**

Hundreds	Tens	Ones
3	7	2
2	8	4
6	5	6

2. 836 + 147 = **983**

Hundreds	Tens	Ones
8	3	6
1	4	7
9	8	3

3. 484 + 371 = **855**

Hundreds	Tens	Ones
4	8	4
3	7	1
8	5	5

4. 183 + 740 = **923**

Hundreds	Tens	Ones
1	8	3
7	4	0
9	2	3

NAME _____

Subtraction in 1,000

Dry-Erase

Use the dry-erase place value chart to create and solve three-digit subtraction problems.

Practice Mode

Use the place value charts to help you subtract and solve these problems.

1. 836 − 371 = **465**

Hundreds	Tens	Ones
8	3	6
3	7	1
4	6	5

2. 371 − 167 = **204**

Hundreds	Tens	Ones
3	7	1
1	6	7
2	0	4

3. 937 − 226 = **711**

Hundreds	Tens	Ones
9	3	7
2	2	6
7	1	1

4. 841 − 173 = **668**

Hundreds	Tens	Ones
8	4	1
1	7	3
6	6	8

Multistep Word Problems

Practice Mode

Decide when to add and subtract to solve these real-life problems.

1. There are 284 students at the elementary school who play sports. There are 491 students who are in a school club. The remaining students play an instrument. If there are 906 students at the school, how many students play an instrument?

   131 students

2. The gym at the school can hold 500 students at one time. If there are 138 kindergartners in the gym along with 208 first graders, how many second graders can come into the gym?

   154 students

3. There are 187 boys and 154 girls in second grade. There are 126 second grade students in one hallway. How many second grade students are in the other hallway?

   215 students

4. The elementary school has 840 desks. 283 of those desks are broken, so the school buys 372 new desks. How many desks does the school have now?

   929 desks

A Closer Look

Make sure to talk positively about math with your child. Be careful to avoid saying, "Some people just aren't good at math," or "Math is hard." Instead, encourage your child to have fun with math and reward effort. Let your child know that practice and hard work build understanding and growth. You may want to share a picture book that celebrates math, such as *On Beyond a Million: An Amazing Math Journey* by David M. Schwartz.

Measuring in Inches

Dry-Erase

Draw these objects beside the dry-erase ruler: a 2-inch caterpillar, a 7-inch snake.

Practice Mode

Write the length of each item.

1.

   2 in.

2.

   5 in.

3. **1** in.

4. **4** in.

Measuring in Centimeters

Dry-Erase

Draw these objects beside the dry-erase ruler: a 7-centimeter bug, a 3-centimeter fish.

Practice Mode

Write the length of each item.

1. **8** cm

2. SOAP

   7 cm

3. FLOSS

   4 cm

4.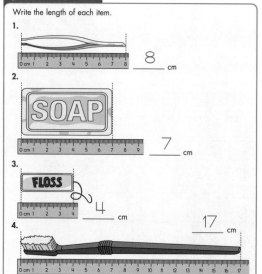

   17 cm

Comparing Units of Measurement

Dry-Erase

Use the dry-erase ruler to compare inches and centimeters. Which unit is shorter and which unit is longer? How many inches and centimeters are equal to each other? Beside the ruler, draw something 10 centimeters or 4 inches long.

Practice Mode

Tell the length of each item to the closest centimeter and inch.

1. **8** centimeters
   3 inches

2. **5** centimeters
   2 inches

3. **13** centimeters
   5 inches

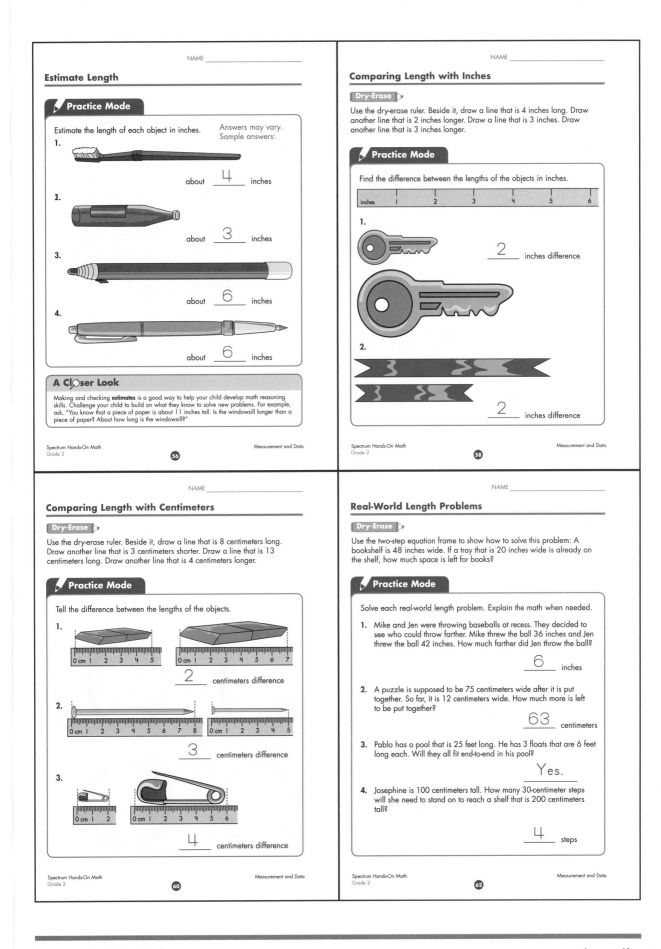

Estimate Length

Practice Mode

Estimate the length of each object in inches.

Answers may vary. Sample answers:

1. about __4__ inches

2. about __3__ inches

3. about __6__ inches

4. about __6__ inches

A Closer Look

Making and checking **estimates** is a good way to help your child develop math reasoning skills. Challenge your child to build on what they know to solve new problems. For example, ask, "You know that a piece of paper is about 11 inches tall. Is the windowsill longer than a piece of paper? About how long is the windowsill?"

Measurement and Data

Comparing Length with Inches

Dry-Erase

Use the dry-erase ruler. Beside it, draw a line that is 4 inches long. Draw another line that is 2 inches longer. Draw a line that is 3 inches. Draw another line that is 3 inches longer.

Practice Mode

Find the difference between the lengths of the objects in inches.

1. __2__ inches difference

2. __2__ inches difference

Measurement and Data

Comparing Length with Centimeters

Dry-Erase

Use the dry-erase ruler. Beside it, draw a line that is 8 centimeters long. Draw another line that is 3 centimeters shorter. Draw a line that is 13 centimeters long. Draw another line that is 4 centimeters longer.

Practice Mode

Tell the difference between the lengths of the objects.

1. __2__ centimeters difference

2. __3__ centimeters difference

3. __4__ centimeters difference

Measurement and Data

Real-World Length Problems

Dry-Erase

Use the two-step equation frame to show how to solve this problem: A bookshelf is 48 inches wide. If a tray that is 20 inches wide is already on the shelf, how much space is left for books?

Practice Mode

Solve each real-world length problem. Explain the math when needed.

1. Mike and Jen were throwing baseballs at recess. They decided to see who could throw farther. Mike threw the ball 36 inches and Jen threw the ball 42 inches. How much farther did Jen throw the ball?

   __6__ inches

2. A puzzle is supposed to be 75 centimeters wide after it is put together. So far, it is 12 centimeters wide. How much more is left to be put together?

   __63__ centimeters

3. Pablo has a pool that is 25 feet long. He has 3 floats that are 6 feet long each. Will they all fit end-to-end in his pool?

   Yes.

4. Josephine is 100 centimeters tall. How many 30-centimeter steps will she need to stand on to reach a shelf that is 200 centimeters tall?

   __4__ steps

Measurement and Data

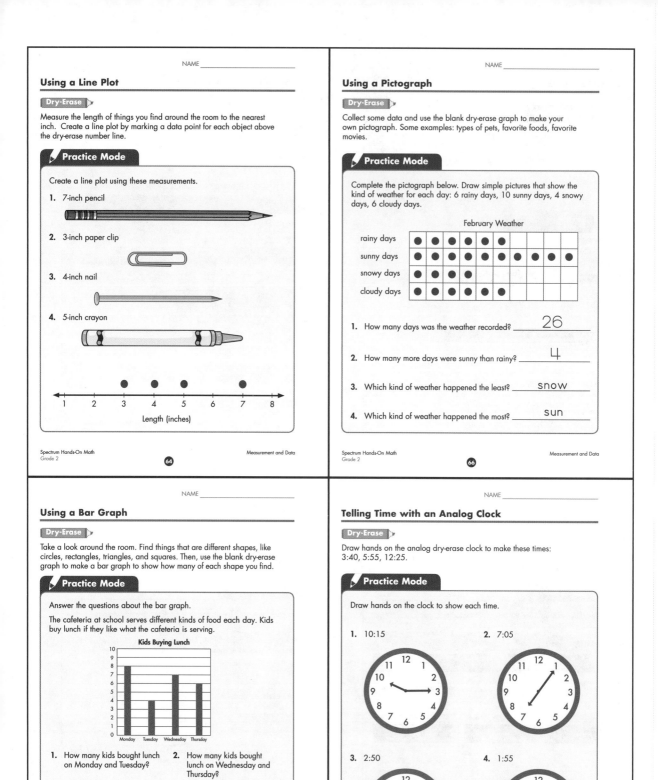

Using a Line Plot

Dry-Erase

Measure the length of things you find around the room to the nearest inch. Create a line plot by marking a data point for each object above the dry-erase number line.

Practice Mode

Create a line plot using these measurements.

1. 7-inch pencil

2. 3-inch paper clip

3. 4-inch nail

4. 5-inch crayon

Length (inches)

Using a Pictograph

Dry-Erase

Collect some data and use the blank dry-erase graph to make your own pictograph. Some examples: types of pets, favorite foods, favorite movies.

Practice Mode

Complete the pictograph below. Draw simple pictures that show the kind of weather for each day: 6 rainy days, 10 sunny days, 4 snowy days, 6 cloudy days.

February Weather

rainy days
sunny days
snowy days
cloudy days

1. How many days was the weather recorded? _____ 26 _____

2. How many more days were sunny than rainy? _____ 4

3. Which kind of weather happened the least? _____ snow _____

4. Which kind of weather happened the most? _____ sun

Using a Bar Graph

Dry-Erase

Take a look around the room. Find things that are different shapes, like circles, rectangles, triangles, and squares. Then, use the blank dry-erase graph to make a bar graph to show how many of each shape you find.

Practice Mode

Answer the questions about the bar graph.

The cafeteria at school serves different kinds of food each day. Kids buy lunch if they like what the cafeteria is serving.

Kids Buying Lunch

Monday Tuesday Wednesday Thursday

1. How many kids bought lunch on Monday and Tuesday?

_____ 12 _____

2. How many kids bought lunch on Wednesday and Thursday?

_____ 13 _____

3. Which day had the most kids buying lunch?

_____ Monday _____

4. What is the difference between the most popular lunch day and the least?

_____ 4 _____

Telling Time with an Analog Clock

Dry-Erase

Draw hands on the analog dry-erase clock to make these times:
3:40, 5:55, 12:25.

Practice Mode

Draw hands on the clock to show each time.

1. 10:15

2. 7:05

3. 2:50

4. 1:55

Telling Time with a Digital Clock

Dry-Erase ▶

Show the times on the digital dry-erase clock: 8:20, 2:30, 7:45.

⬤ Practice Mode

Show the time from the analog clock on the digital clock.

1.

5:30

2.

6:55

3.

2:30

4.

12:20

Spectrum Hands-On Math
Grade 2

Measurement and Data

Adding and Subtracting with Dollars and Coins

Dry-Erase ▶

Solve the problem on the dry-erase pad. Draw the money you have left.
You have $1.00 to spend at the store. You spend 25¢ on a piece of gum
and 50¢ on a pack of crackers. How much money do you have left?

⬤ Practice Mode

Add or subtract to find how many dollars and cents you have.

1. 25¢ 10¢ 10¢ 10¢ 5¢ 5¢

1 quarter + 3 dimes + 2 nickles   65¢

2. $1   25¢   25¢   25¢

1 dollar   + 3 quarters $1.75

3. 3 dimes + 6 quarters ___$1.80___

4. 2 dollars – 2 quarters – 5 dimes ___$1.00___

5. 1 dollar + 6 nickels – 1 quarter ___$1.05___

6. 10 dimes + 4 quarters ___$2.00___

Spectrum Hands-On Math
Grade 2

Measurement and Data

Money Word Problems

⬤ Practice Mode

Add and subtract to find the answers to the word problems.

$1   25¢   10¢   5¢   1¢

1. Jada has 3 dollars, 4 quarters, 6 dimes, and 7 pennies. If she buys
a bag of chips for $1.45, how much money will she have left?

   $3.22

2. Malik goes to the store with $7.82. He buys candy for $2.15
and juice for $1.59. How much money will Malik have left?

   $4.08

3. Tiana has $4.00. She wants to buy a book that costs $3.50 and
a toy that costs $2.75. How much more money will Tiana need to
buy the book and the toy?

   $2.25

A Closer Look

If you often use a debit or credit card to make purchases, your child may be unfamiliar with
using cash. Foster math skills by allowing your child to buy things at the store using bills and
coins. Encourage your child to verify that the right amount of change was given. You may wish
to provide a small cash allowance for your child that encourages thinking about spending
and saving.

Spectrum Hands-On Math
Grade 2

Measurement and Data

Quadrilaterals

Dry-Erase ▶

Use the dry-erase dot grid to draw quadrilaterals.

⬤ Practice Mode

Color the quadrilaterals.

Spectrum Hands-On Math
Grade 2

Geometry

Spectrum Hands-On Math
Grade 2

Answer Key

Other Shapes

Dry-Erase ▷

Use the dry-erase dot grid to draw one of each: triangle, pentagon, hexagon, cube.

Practice Mode

Fill in the missing information for each shape.

1. triangle: 3 _sides_, 3 angles

2. cube: 3-D shape, 6 _square_ faces

3. _pentagon_: 5 sides, 5 angles

4. hexagon: 6 _sides_, 6 _angles_

Draw the shapes.

5. hexagon   6. triangle

Label the shapes.

7.   8.

cube   _hexagon_

Area Concepts

Dry-Erase ▷

Use the dry-erase dot grid to draw rectangles of different sizes. Then, use the dots to draw equal size squares inside each rectangle and tell how many squares fit.

Practice Mode

Solve the multiplication problems. Count the total number of squares for help. The first one has been done for you.

1.    6 $2 \times 3 = 6$

2. 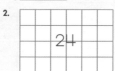   24 $6 \times 4 = $ _24_

3. 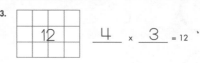   12   _4_ $\times$ _3_ $= 12$

4.    10   _5_ $\times$ _2_ $= 10$

Fractions with Circles

Dry-Erase ▷

Draw a circle on the dry-erase pad. Draw lines through the circle to make fractions. Name the fractions.

Practice Mode

Shade each circle as described.

1. Show $\frac{3}{4}$.   2. Show $\frac{1}{2}$.

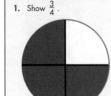   

3. Show $\frac{1}{3}$.   4. Show $\frac{3}{3}$.

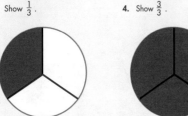

Fractions with Rectangles

Dry-Erase ▷

Draw a rectangle on the dry-erase pad. Draw lines through the rectangle to divide it equally into fractions. Name the fractions.

Practice Mode

Shade each rectangle as described.

1. Show $\frac{1}{3}$.   2. Show $\frac{3}{4}$.

3. Show $\frac{2}{4}$.   4. Show $\frac{2}{2}$.

Write the fraction each rectangle is showing.

5. 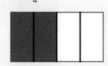 $\frac{2}{3}$ 6. $\frac{1}{2}$

Number Cards

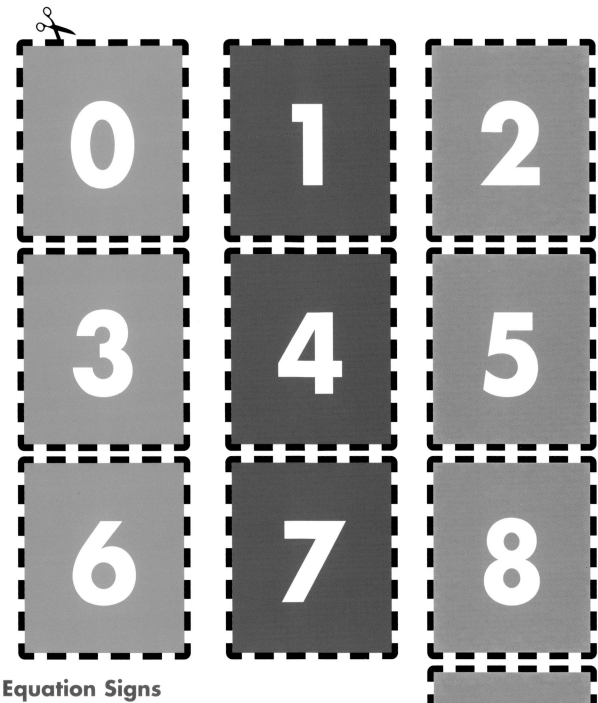

0 1 2
3 4 5
6 7 8
9

Equation Signs

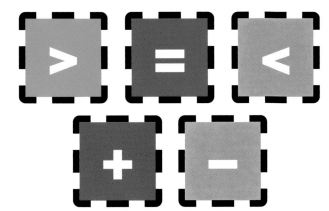

> = <
+ −

Number Cards

0 1 2

3 4 5

6 7 8

Shape Cut-Outs

9

Number Cards

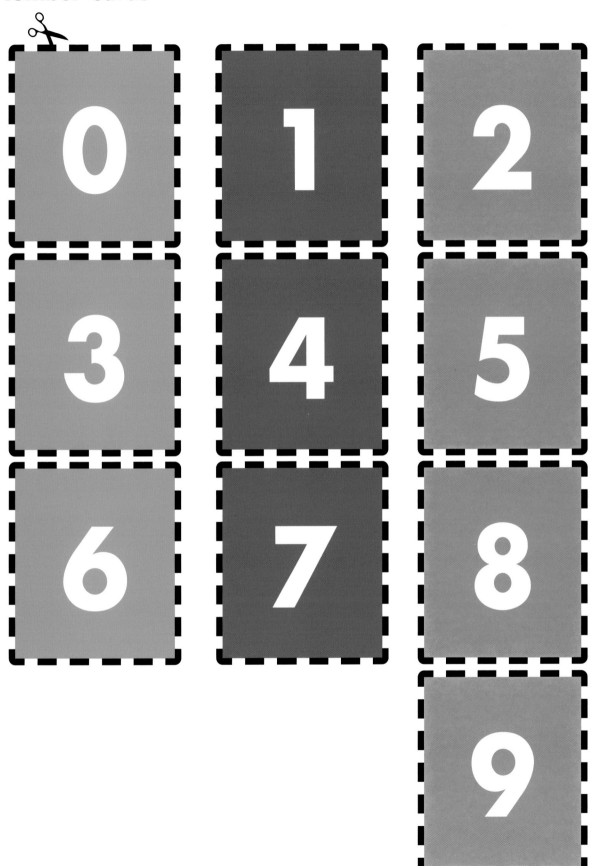

Apple Counters

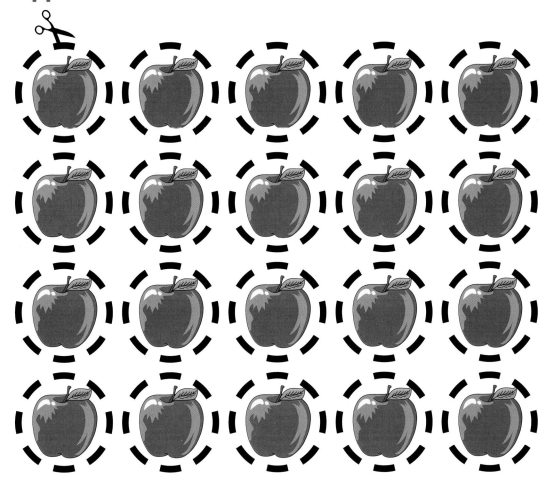

Square Counters

Frog Hopper

Car Cut-Outs

Base-Ten Cookies (Chips)

Rectangle Cut-Outs

Ruler Cut-Out

Base-Ten Blocks

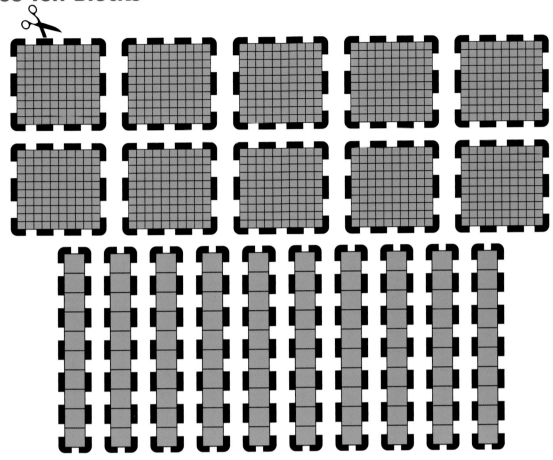

Base-Ten Cookies

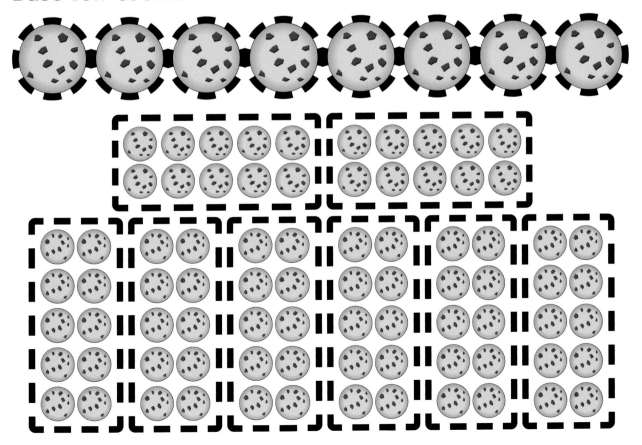

Circle Fraction Cut-Outs

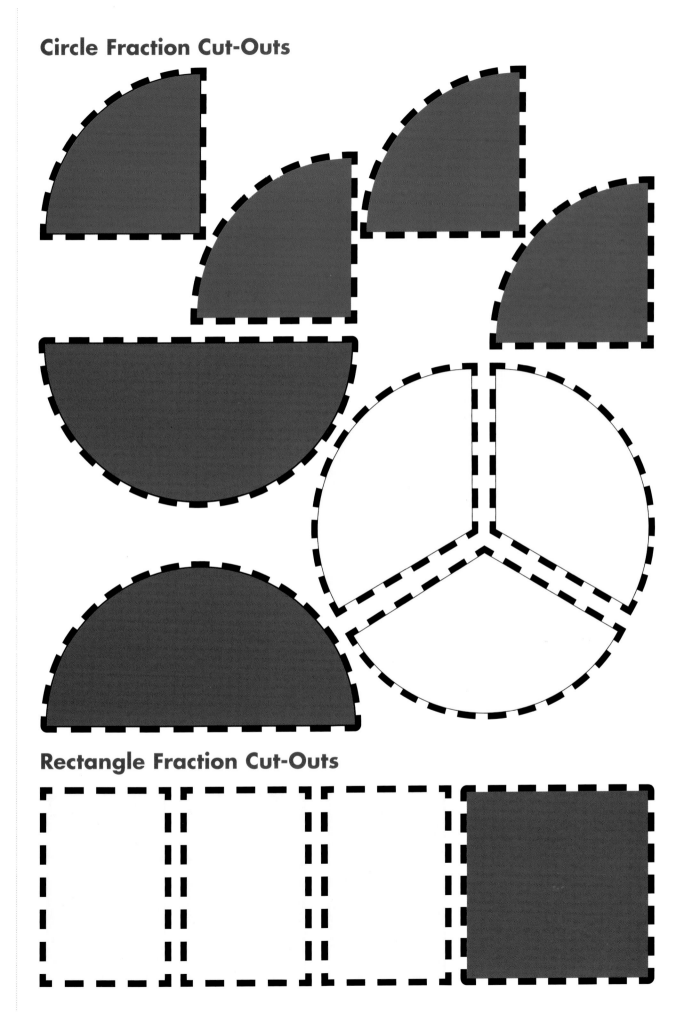

Rectangle Fraction Cut-Outs

Rectangle Fraction Cut-Outs

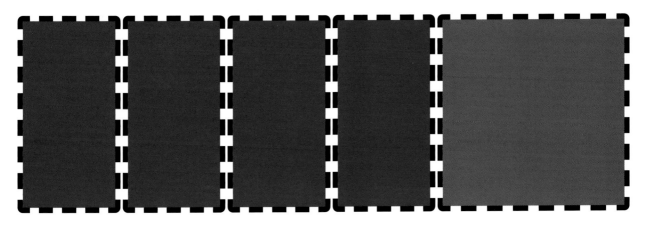

Frog Cut-Outs

Star Cut-Outs

Shape Cut-Outs

Object Cut-Outs

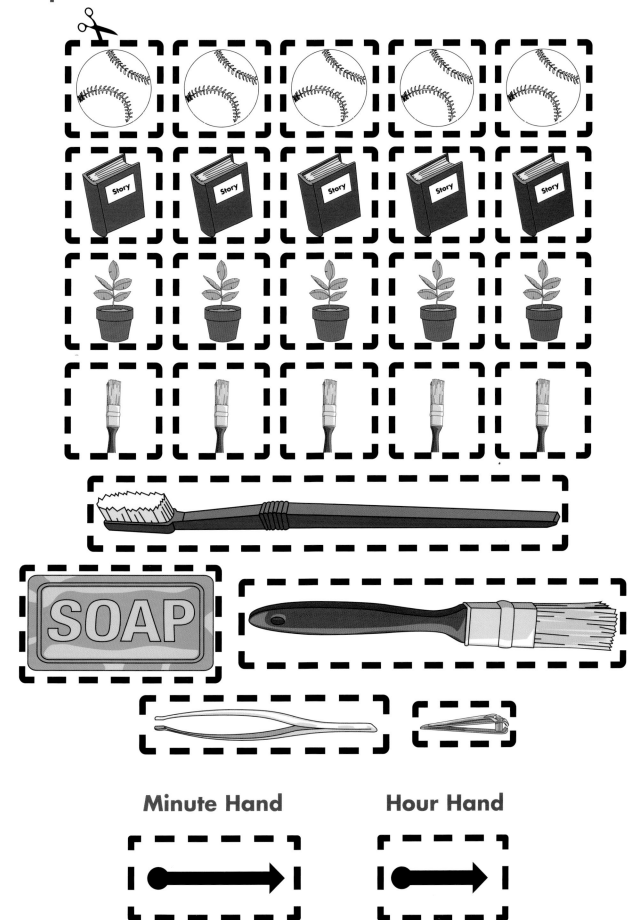

Minute Hand

Hour Hand

Money Cut-Outs

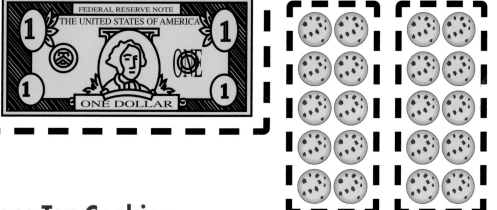

Base-Ten Cookies

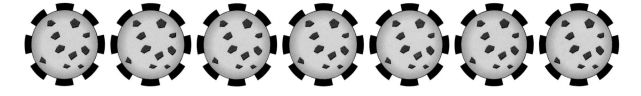

Cube Net

Fold at the dotted lines and use tape to put together.

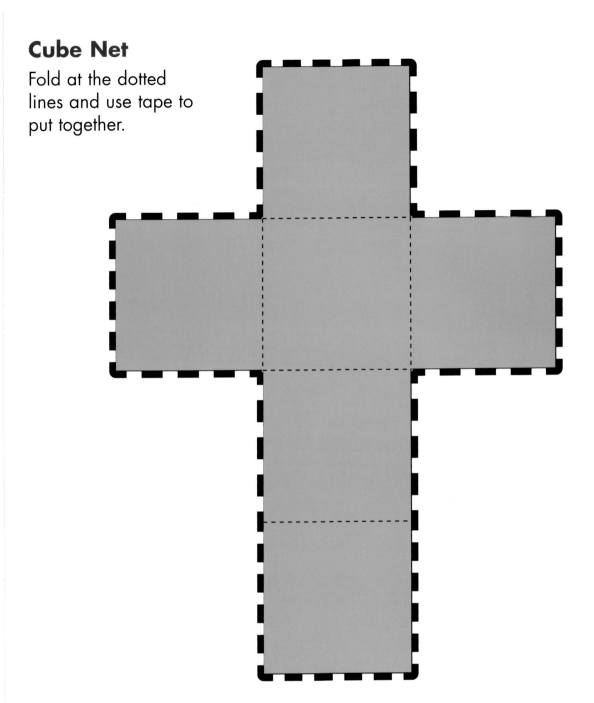

Base-Ten Blocks (Ones Blocks)

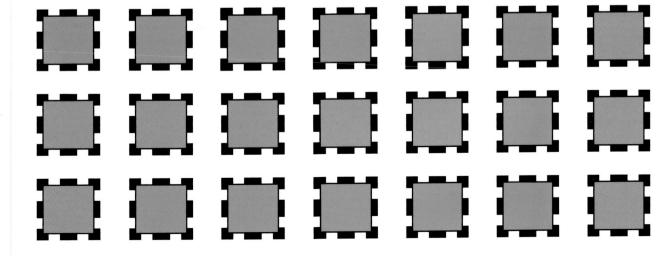